I0110618

# 武器陌圖

# 200 Diagrams
## Of Samurai Weapons & Equipment
A pictorial & historical guide

**Translated & Explained by Jack Chen Jiayi**

**Originally written in 1848, by Kobayashi Sukemichi**

Copyright © 2017 by Chen Jiayi

All rights reserved. This book or any portion thereof may not be reproduced or used in any manner whatsoever without the express written permission of the publisher except for the use of brief quotations in a book review or scholarly journal.

First Printing: 2017

ISBN 978-981-11-5408-9

Chen Jiayi
http://www.SamuraiBookShop.com/
http://www.Gekiken.org/

*In dedication to the bravery and wisdom
of Men before us.*


*For my grandparents.*

# Contents

# Preface

武器䑛圖 (*buki nihyaku zu*) is a rare antique Japanese book that documented the various weapons of war in colorful drawings. It was written in the 1st year of Kaei (1848) by Kobayashi Sukemichi.

It serves as a comprehensive and accurate historical reference for us to know what are the names and pictures of Samurai weapons.

I was fortunate enough to obtain a real antique copy in my hands. Though it was badly eaten by bookworms, I've made it my mission to restore, translate and spread this incredible and precious resource to the world.

Sincerely,
Jack Chen Jiayi

www.SamuraiBookshop.com
www.Gekiken.org

*Buki Nihyaku Zu* is quite a large antique book. Compared to most others which are about A5 size, this book is approximately A4 size. It consists of 32 pages, of which 25 pages are the main content, containing the drawings of different weapons and their names.

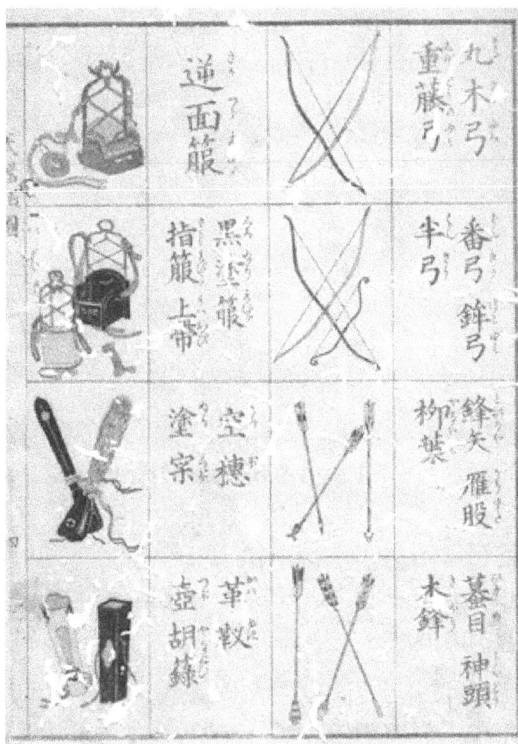

A page from the antique book

The drawings organized neatly in a table format with 16 cells, as you can see above. On the left is the drawing, and on the right are the weapons' names. A drawing may contain more than 1 weapon/tool.

Although there are 200 drawings total, there are in fact more than 400 weapons/tools being named here! We will be going through every single item or weapon in this book.

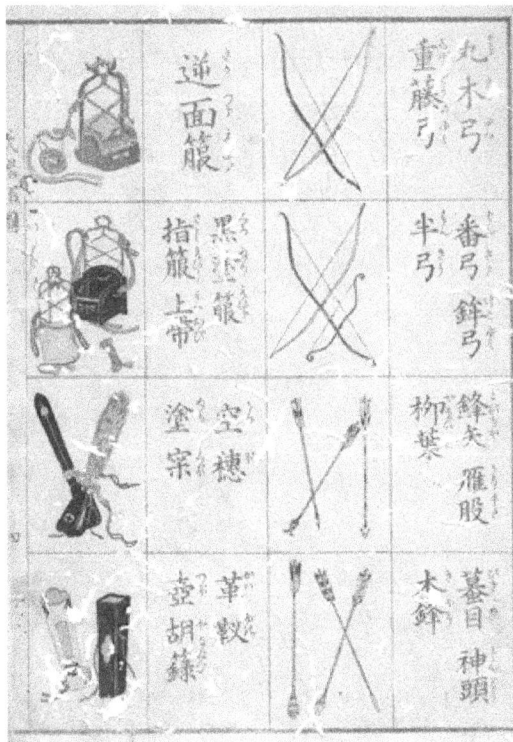

**Page 1 of the Drawings**

**Drawing #1**

## 1) 丸木弓 (*maruki yumi*)

This is the lighter-colored bow in the diagram, asymmetrical design, made from tree limbs.

## 2) 重籘弓 (*shigedo no yumi*)

This is the darker-colored bow, made by wrapping it with heavy rattan.

———————————————

**Drawing #2**

## 3) 番弓 (*bankyu*)

War bow.

## 4) 半弓 (*hankyu*)

Literally "half bow". A shorter variation of the normal length bow.

## 5) 鉾弓 (*hoko yumi*)

Literally "Spear Bow". Notice the middle bow has a bladed tip.

6) 鏃矢 (*tokari ya*)
Right-most; pointed arrow.

7) 雁股 (*karimata*)
Middle; forked arrow-head.

8) 柳葉 (*yanaiba*)
Left; willow-leaf arrow-head.

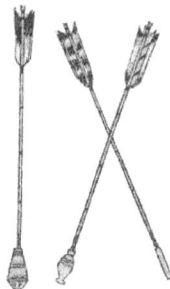

**Drawing #3**

9) 蟇目 (*hikime*)
Whistling turnip-shaped arrow-head.

10) 神頭 (*jindou*)
Fat-head arrow.

11) 木鏃 (*kihou*)
Wooden tip arrow.

**Drawing #4**

12) 逆面箙
(*gyaku men ebira*)
Rear view of quiver.

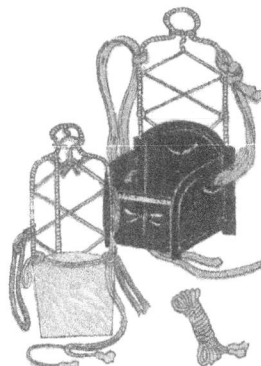

**Drawing #5**

13) 黒塗箙
(*kuro nuri ebira*)
Top; Black painted quiver.

14) 指箙 (*sashi ebira*)
Left; Quiver, where arrows are sashed in.

15) 上帯 (*uwa obi*)
Bottom; An outer sash worn by Samurai.

**Drawing #6**

16) 空穂 (*utsubo*)
*Utsubo* style of quiver.

17) 塗窠
(*nuri utsubo*)
Left; Black lacquered version.

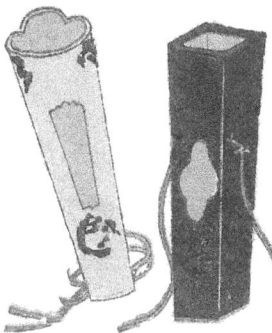

**Drawing #7**

18) 革靫 (*kawa yuki*)
Box-shaped quiver.

19) 壺胡籙
(*tsubo yanaguhi*)
Tube-shaped quiver.

**Drawing #8**

# Page 2: Archery Related Equipment

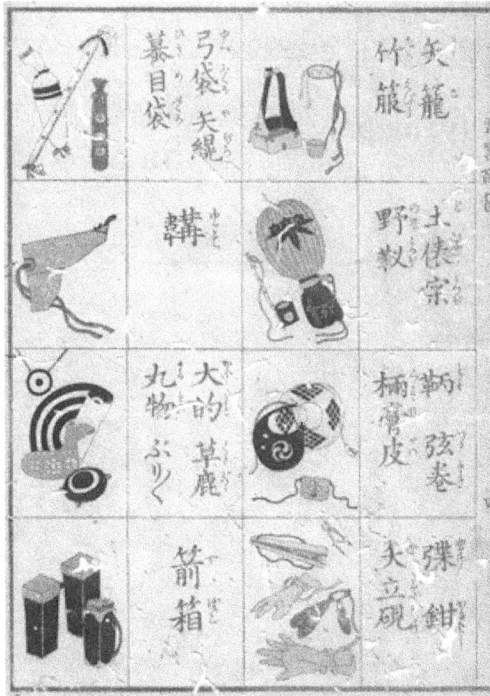

**Page 2 of the Drawings**

**Drawing #9**

20) 矢籠 (*shiko*)
Arrow basket.

21) 竹箙 (*take ebira*)
Bamboo quiver.

**Drawing #10**

22) 土俵窠
(*dohyou utsubo*)
Right; Quiver with a large basket that resembles a sandbag.

23) 野靫 (*no utsubo*)
Field quiver.

**Drawing #11**

24) 鞆 (*tomo*)
Left; Archer's left-wrist protector.

25) 弦巻 (*tsuru maki*)
Reel for a spare bowstring.

26) 裲膏皮
(*uchi kou kawa*)
Bottom; Red pouch.

**Drawing #12**

27) 䩫 (*yugake*)
Archer's glove.

28) 鉗 (*tsugumi*)
Top; Forceps.

29) 矢立硯
(*yatate suzuri*)
Top-left; Portable brush-and-ink case.

**30) 弓袋**
**(*yumi bukuro*)**
Cloth bag for the bow.

**31) 矢縄 (*yaburo*)**
Cloth bag for arrows.

**32) 蕪目袋**
**(*hikime bukuro*)**
Cloth bag shaped like a turnip.

**Drawing #13**

**33) 鞲 (*yugote*)**
Shoulder/arm-wear for archers.

**Drawing #14**

---

**34) 大的 (*oo mato*)**
Literally "big target".

**35) 草鹿 (*kusakado*)**
Archery target in the shape of a deer.

**36) 丸物**
**(*maru mono*)**
Top-left; Round object (for target practice).

**37) ぶりく (*buriku*)**
Information not found.

**Drawing #15**

**38) 箭箱 (*yabako*)**
Arrows chest.

**Drawing #16**

# Page 3: Swords

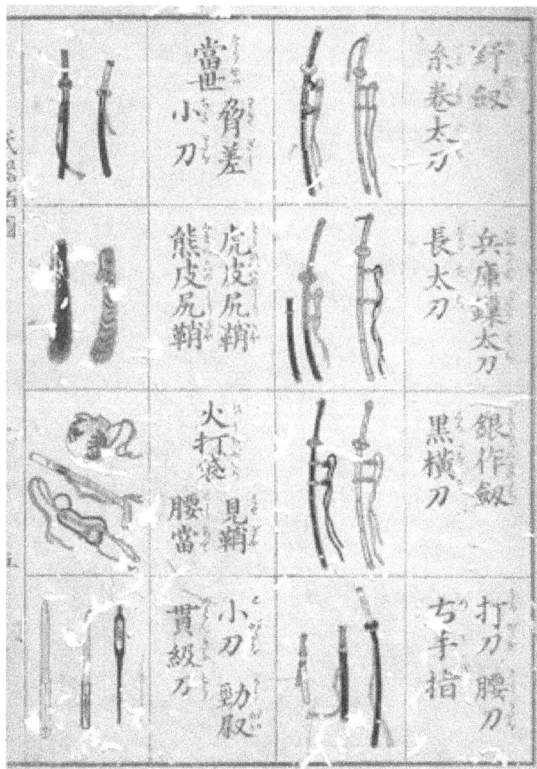

**Page 3 of the Drawings**

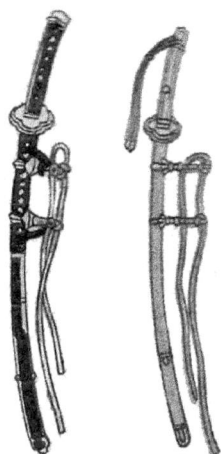

**39) 野劍 (*nodachi*)**
Right; Field sword.

**40) 糸巻太刀
(*itomaki tachi*)**
Left; Fabric-wrapped (hilt and upper section of the sheath) sword.

**Drawing #17**

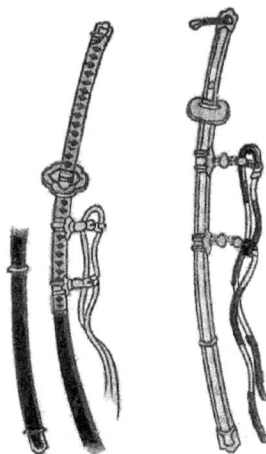

**41) 兵庫鑕太刀
(*hyogo gusari tachi*)**
Right; The sheath is attached to the rope via metal chains (*kusari*).

**42) 長太刀
(*naga tachi*)**
Left; Long sword.

**Drawing #18**

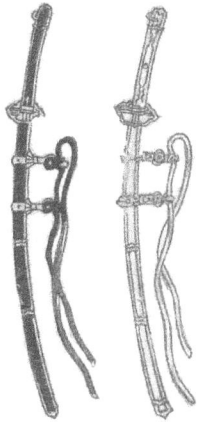

43) 銀作劔 **(shirogane zukuri no tachi)**
Right; Silver sword.

44) 黒横刀 **(kuro tachi)**
Left; Black lacquered sword.

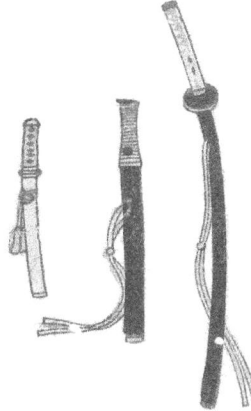

**Drawing #19**

45) 打刀 **(uchigatana)**
Right; Shorter than a "*Tachi*", this is sashed in the belt with the edge up.

46) 腰刀 **(koshigatana)**
Middle; Literally "waist sword".

**Drawing #20**

47) 右手指 **(metezashi)**
Left; Armour piercer, sashed on the right side of the belt. Also 馬手差, or 鎧通し (*yoroi-doshi*).

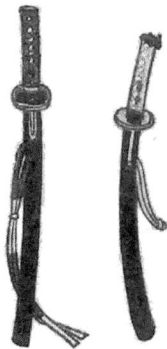

當世 **(tousei)**
Literally "current". This is to say that these 2 weapons are the ones *currently* in use at the time this ancient manual was published.

48) 脅差 **(wakizashi)**
Right; Samurai short sword.

**Drawing #21**

49) 小刀 **(chisagatana)**
Left; Literally short Katana.

50) 虎皮尻鞘 **(tora no kawa no shirizaya)**
Right; Sheath cover made of tiger fur.

51) 熊皮尻鞘 **(kuma no kawa no shirizaya)**
Left; Sheath cover made of bear skin.

**Drawing #22**

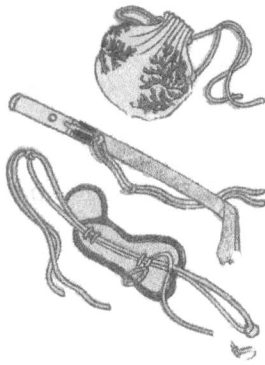

**52) 火打袋 (hiuchi bukuro)**
Top; Flint pouch for fire-making.

**53) 見鞘 (misezaya)**
Middle; Decorative cover for a short blade's sheath.

**Drawing #23**

**54) 腰當 (koshiate)**
Bottom; Worn on the waist. The sword will be hung onto this piece.

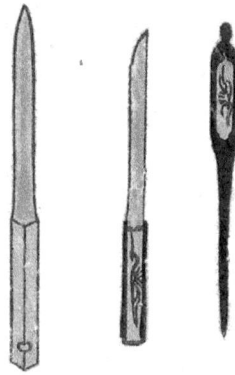

**Drawing #24**

**55) 小刀 (kogatana)**
Small utility blade.

**56) 勁敗 (kogai)**
Right; Spike-like, hair arrangement tool.

**57) 貫級刀 (kankyu tou)**
Left; Blade and hilt made from a single piece of steel.

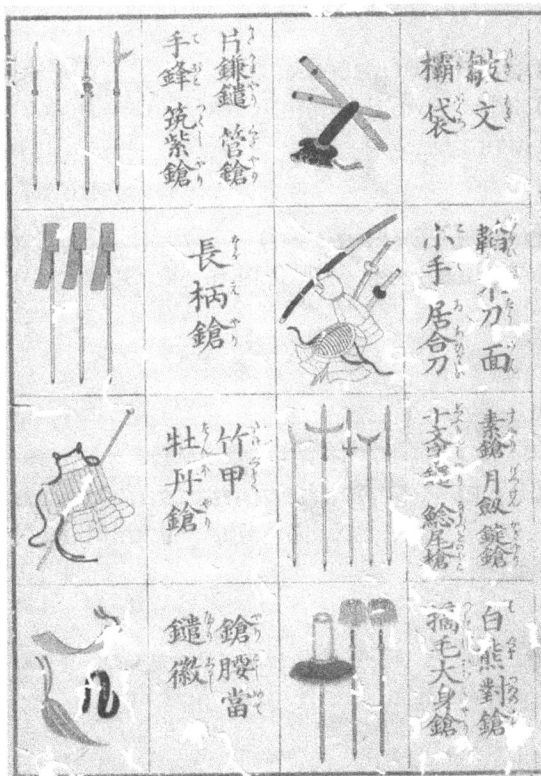

**Page 4 of the Drawings**

**Drawing #25**

## 58) 皺文 (*shibomon*)
Information not found. The nearest is "*shibokawa*", which is a leather sheath for swords. The picture shows 2, so perhaps it is for both the long and short swords.

## 59) 欛袋 (*tsuka bukuro*)
Bottom, black; Cloth cover for sword hilt.

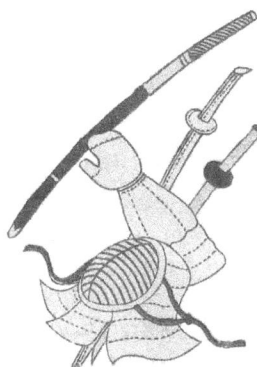

**Drawing #26**

## 60) 韜 (*fukuro shinai*)
Middle; Split bamboo wrapped with cloth, for sword fencing practice.

## 61) 木刀 (*bokutou*)
Wooden sword.

## 62) 面 (*men*)
Bottom; fencing mask.

## 63) 小手 (*kote*)
Fencing gauntlets.

## 64) 居合刀 (*iaitou*)
Top; Sword for drawing (*iaijutsu*) practice.

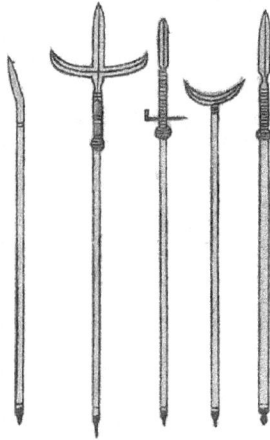

**Drawing #27**

65) 素鎗 (*suyari*)
Right; Literally "plain Spear".

66) 月劔 (*getsuken*)
Right-second; Literally "Moon Sword".

67) 鍵槍 (*kagiyari*)
Middle; Spear with side-hook.

68) 十文字槍 (*jumonji yari*)
Left-second; Cross-bladed Spear.

69) 鯰尾槍 (*namazuo no hoko*)
Left; Interestingly, the Hiragana for 槍 is not "*yari*", but "*hoko*". Notice that the blade is slanted to one side.

---

**Drawing #28**

70) 白熊對槍 (*haguma tsui no yari*)
Right; 2 Spears with white yak tail hair. The word "*tsui*" means a paired set.

71) 摘毛大身槍 (*tsumige oomi yari*)
Left, Hanging fur long bladed Spear.

---

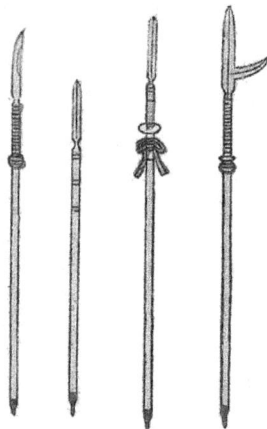

**Drawing #29**

72) 片鎌鎗 (*katakama yari*)
Right; Spear with a side blade.

73) 管鎗 (*kuda yari*)
Right-second; Sliding Spear. Has a tube which your front hand will grip on, for easy sliding.

74) 手鉾 (*teboko*)
Left-second; Read also "*teyari*", a shorter variant of Spear, more suitable for urban areas.

75) 筑紫槍 (*tsukushi yari*)
Left; Read also "*kikuchi yari*". Spear with a single cutting edge.

## 76) 長柄槍
**(*nagae yari*)**
Long shaft Spear.

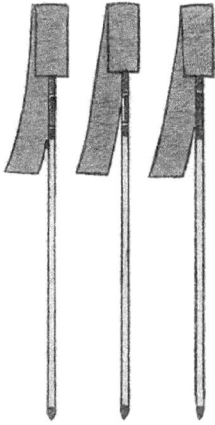

**Drawing #30**

## 77) 竹甲
**(*take gusoku*)**
Literally, "bamboo armour". Notice the protection is only for the wearer's left-side, and leaves the right-side more exposed.

**Drawing #31**

## 78) 牡舟槍
**(*botan yari*)**
Spear with a padded tip for fencing practice.

---

## 79) 槍腰當
**(*yari koshiate*)**
Right, Black; Tied to a Samurai's belt. Supposedly as a holster for Spears.

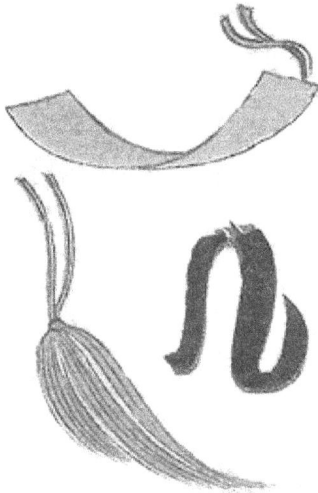

## 80) 鑓徽
**(*yari jirushi*)**
Top & Bottom-Left; Symbol or emblem that can be tied to Spears.

**Drawing #32**

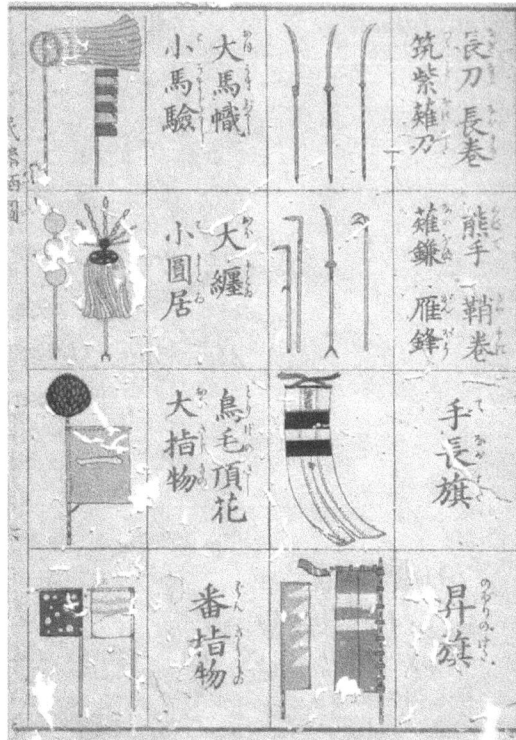

**Page 5 of the Drawings**

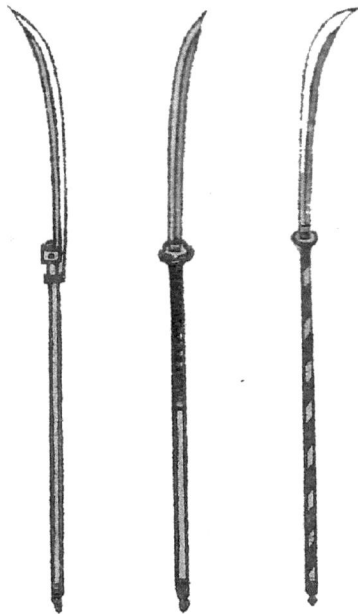

**Drawing #33**

## 81) 長刀 (*naginata*)
Right; Polearm with a single-edged curved blade.

## 82) 長巻 (*nagamaki*)
Middle; blade is like a Japanese sword, but with a much longer handle.

## 83) 筑紫薙刀
(*tsukushi naginata*)
Left; Normally, blades have a 'tang' that is inserted into the handle. But here, there is no tang, and the blade is externally fixed onto the shaft.

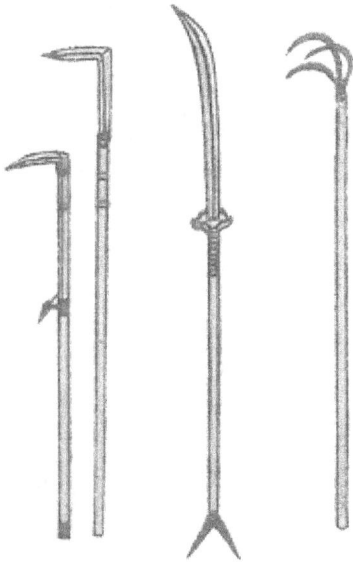

**Drawing #34**

## 84) 熊手 (*kumade*)
Right; Literally "bear's paws".

## 85) 鞘巻 (*sayamaki*)
Right-second; Literally "sheath wrapping".

## 86) 薙鎌 (*nagigama*)
Left-second; Literally "Mowing Sickle".

## 87) 雁鋒 (*ganboko*)
Left-second; Literally "Goose Spear".

---

## 88) 手長旗 (*tenaga hata*)
Literally "Long-armed Flag".

Notice that the top of the flag is written 八幡大菩薩, which is the Japanese God of War.

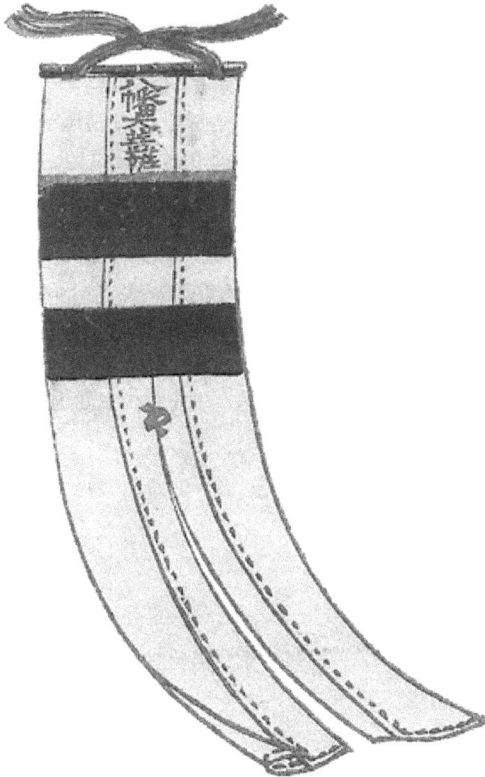

**Drawing #35**

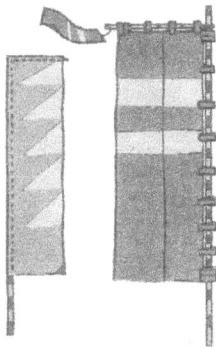

**89) 昇旗**
**(nobori no hata)**
Literally "Rising Flag". The flag is attached to a pole with a cross-rod, so that it is visible even when there is no wind.

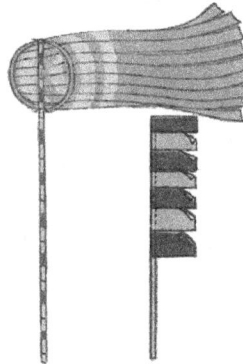

**Drawing #36**

**90) 大馬幟**
**(oo uma jirushi)**
An "uma jirushi" is a flag carried in battle to identify an important military commander. This is the big version.

**Drawing #37**

**91) 小馬験**
**(ko uma jirushi)**
This is the smaller version. Notice that the last character is read the same as "jirushi" even though they are written differently.

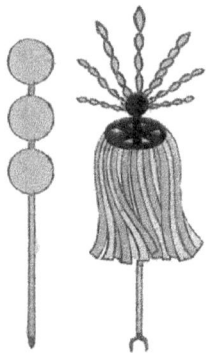

**92) 大纏**
**(oo matoi)**
Right; This is a flag to show the General's location in the battlefield.

**Drawing #38**

**93) 小圓居**
**(ko matoi)**
A smaller version. Notice that the characters are different, but read the same.

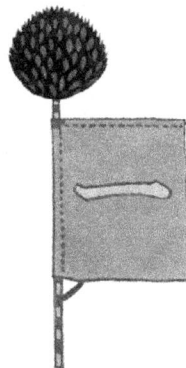

**94) 鳥毛頂花**
**(torige no chouka)**
A decorative bird-feathers piece on the top of a flag.

**Drawing #39**

**95) 大指物**
**(oo sashimono)**
"Sashimono" is a flag worn by soldiers on their back in battle. "Oo" means it's a big version.

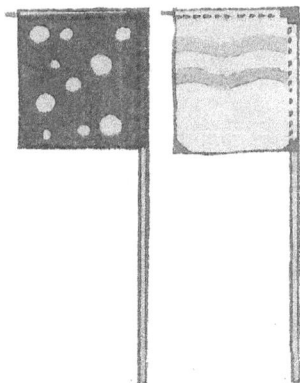

**96) 番指物**
**(ban sashimono)**
Similarly worn on the back by soldiers in battle, but this one identifies their "ban" (guard) division.

**Drawing #40**

**Page 6 of the Drawings**

**Drawing #41**

**Drawing #42**

97) 番小指
**(ban kozashi)**
Right; Same as "*ban sashimono*" previously, but this is a smaller version.

98) 腰指
**(koshi zashi)**
Left; Instead of wearing on the back like the previous, this flag is worn on the waist.

99) 袖印
**(sode jirushi)**
Bottom; This is an identification badge worn by Samurai on their shoulder.

100) 笠標
**(kasa jirushi)**
Top; Similarly an identification badge, but worn on the head.

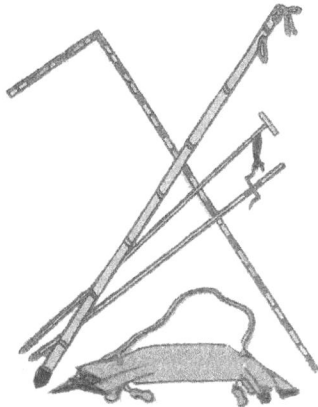

## 101) 旗竿 (*hata zao*)
Long pole for flags or banners.

## 102) 幡袋
(*hata bukuro*)
Bottom; A cloth bag for storing the flags or banners.

## 103) 列子杖
(*sekozue*)
Middle; Information not found. **列子** is also written as "*resshi*", who is a historical Chinese figure. "*zue*" means a cane or staff.

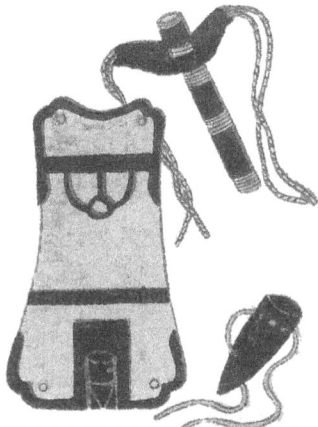

**Drawing #43**

---

## 104) 枇杷板 (*biwa ita*)
A long board which extends along the top of a wall plate.

## 105) 請筒 (*ukezutsu*)
This is a holder for the flag pole (*sashimono*).

## 106) 蜘手 (*kumode*)
Similar to 84) "*kumade*", these are grappling iron tools.

## 107) 柄立革 (*tsukatate gawa*)
Leather used in supporting the flag-pole holder.

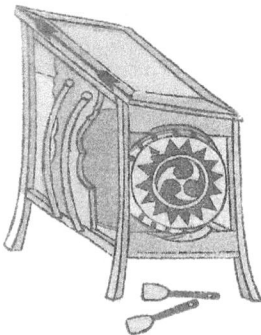

**Drawing #44**

---

## 108) 太鼓
(*taiko*)
Taiko drum.

**Drawing #45**

## 109) 半鐘 (*hanshou*)
Right; Fire bell.

## 110) 鉦鼓 (*dora*)
Left; Cymbals or gongs used by marching troops.

**Drawing #46**

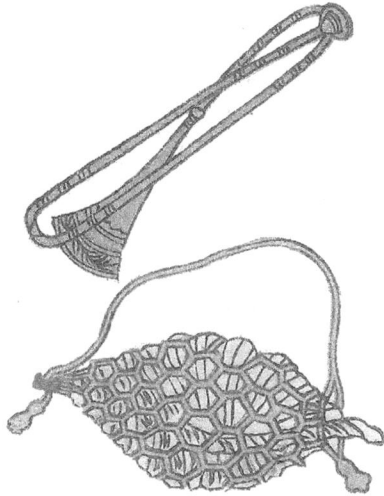

### 111) 貝 (*kai*)

Bottom; Read also "*jinkai*". This is a horn which you blow into, to create sounds for signalling in battlefield.

### 112) 喇叭
### (*torampetto*)

Top; Literally "trumpet". Interestingly, the hiragana reading for this is the English derivation.

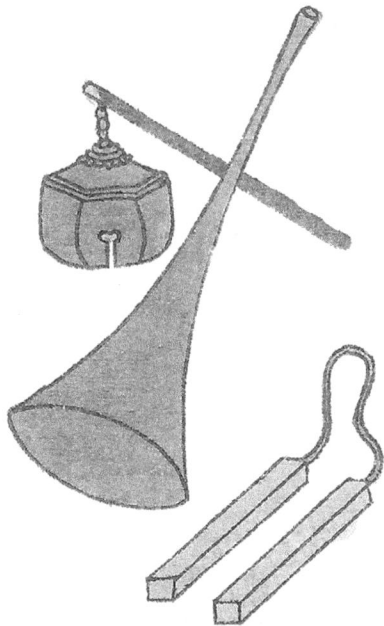

**Drawing #47**

### 113) 傳令管 (*denreikan*)

Middle; Loud-hailer for transmitting military orders.

### 114) 祈 (*inorishigi*)

Bottom; 2 pieces of metal that clanks together, used in making prayers.

### 115) 驛路鈴 (*ekiro no suzu*)

Top; Station bells.
Read more at: https://en.wikipedia.org/wiki/Station_bell

**Drawing #48**

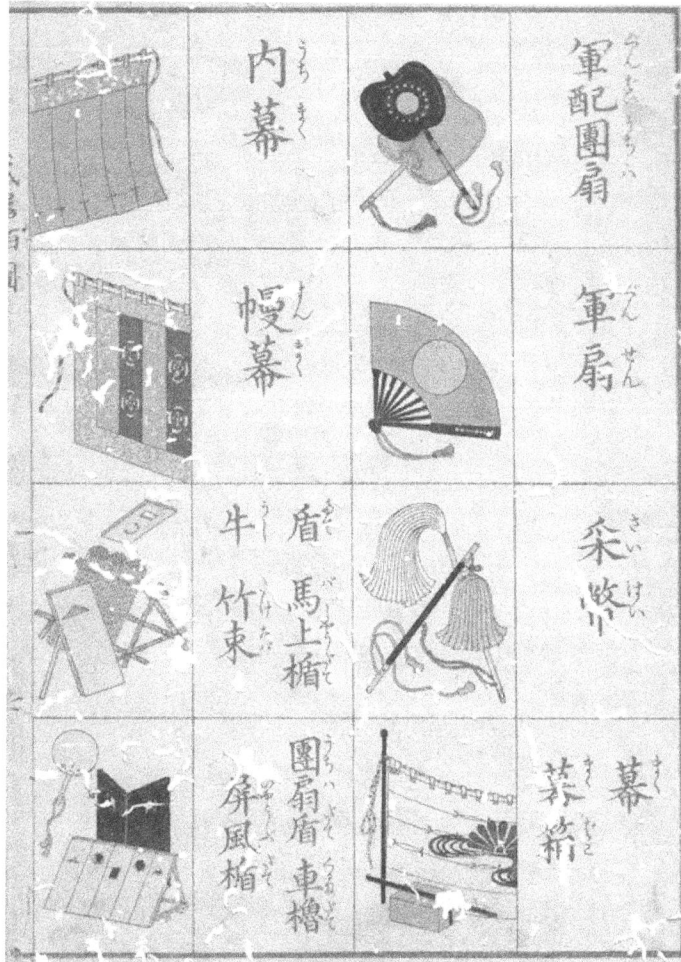

**Page 7 of the Drawings**

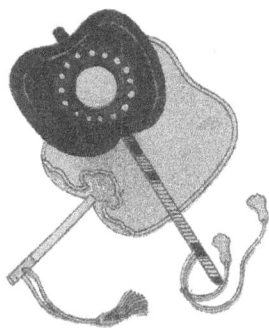

**Drawing #49**

116) 軍配團扇
(*gunbai uchiwa*)
A hard rigid type of
fan, used for
signalling purposes
in the military.

**Drawing #50**

117) 軍扇
(*gunsen*)
Japanese war fan.
Foldable, and used by
soldiers to fan
themselves for
comfort in the
battlefield.

118) 采幣
(*saihai*)
Samurai commander's baton.

**Drawing #51**

119) 幕 (*maku*)
Curtain used in Samurai military encampment.

120) 幕箱
(*makubako*)
Chest for storing the curtain.

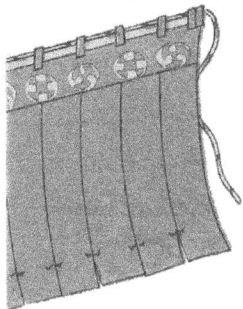

**Drawing #52**

121) 内幕
(*uchimaku*)
Curtains used in the interior sections of the encampment.

**Drawing #53**

122) 慢幕
(*manmaku*)
A curtain that is long horizontally.

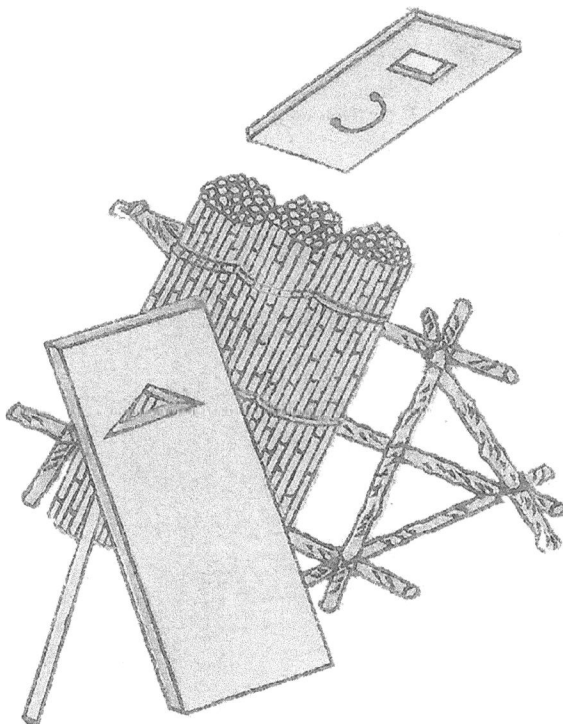

**Drawing #54**

123) 盾
(*tate*)
Bottom; Shield.

124) 馬上楯
(*bajou date*)
Top; A smaller shield, used in one hand while riding on the horse.

125) 牛
(*ushi*)
Frame, for the bamboo wall.

126) 竹束
(*taketaba*)
Bundles of bamboo, used as a defensive wall.

**Drawing #55**

**Drawing #56**

## 127) 團扇盾
### (*uchiwa date*)
Top-left; Shield that looks like 116) "*uchiwa*", and used to block projectiles.

## 128) 車櫓
### (*kuruma yagura*)
Bottom; Wooden defensive frame on wheels.

## 129) 屏風楯
### (*byoubu date*)
Black; Shield wall that's like a folding screen.

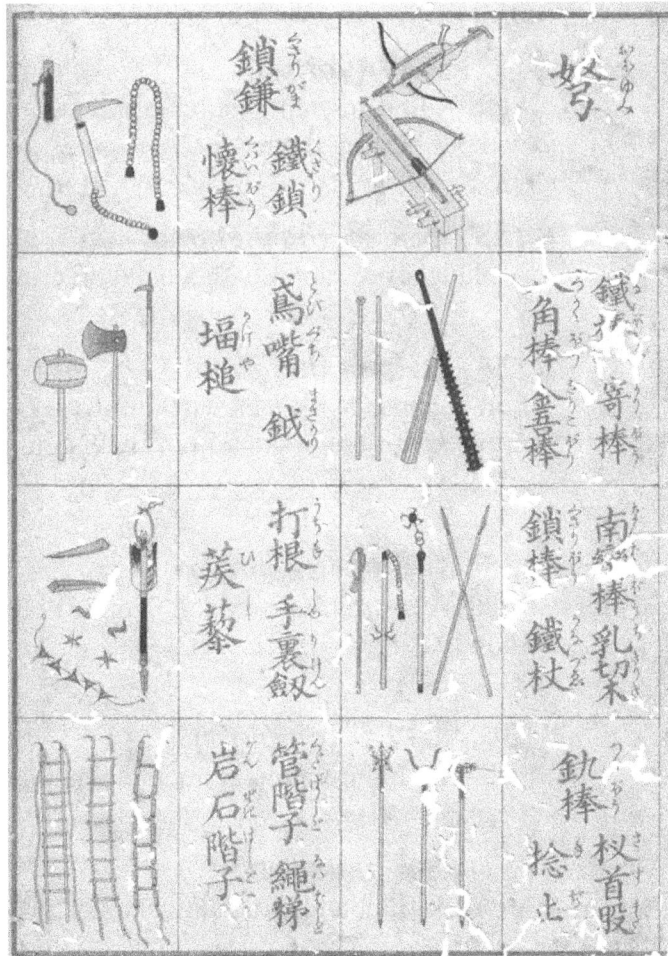

**Page 8 of the Drawings**

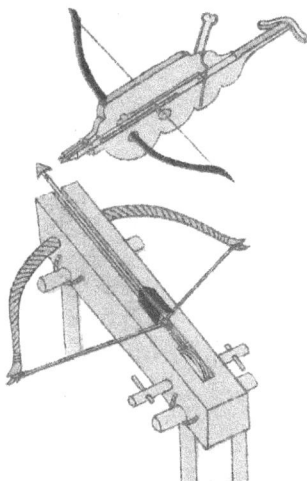

130) 弩
*(ooyumi)*
Crossbow.
Notice that the top one is the Chinese "Repeating Crossbow".

**Drawing #57**

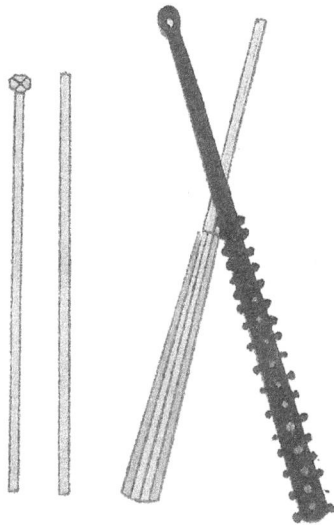

**131) 鐵棒 (tetsubo)**
Metal bludgeon weapon.

**132) 寄棒 (yoribo)**
Left; A Staff meant to subdue and capture an opponent without hurting them.

**133) 八角棒 (hakkakubo)**
A bludgeon weapon with a octagon cross-section.

**134) 金吾棒 (kingobo)**
Left-second; No Japanese info found. But based on Chinese info, "*kingo*" refers to a Staff that is gold painted.

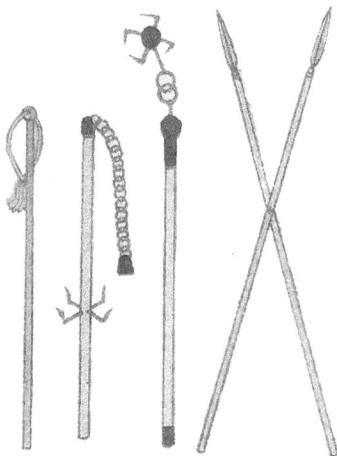

**Drawing #58**

---

**135) 南蛮棒 (nanbanbo)**
Right; A restraining weapon. Notice that the 2 Spears are setup like a pair of scissors.

**136) 乳切木 (chigiriki)**
Flail with hollow pole, retractable metal chain.

**137) 鎖棒 (kusaribo)**
A longer flail, and the chain is not retractable.

**138) 鐵杖 (tetsujo)**
Right; Metal cane.

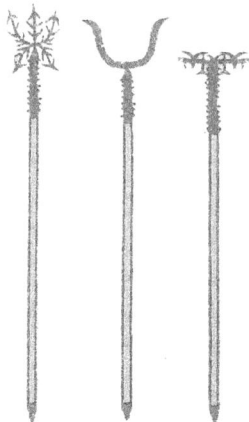

**Drawing #59**

---

**139) 釶棒 (tsukubo)**
Right; T-shaped tool to help capture criminals without harming them. Also: 突棒.

**140) 杈首股 (sasumata)**
Middle; A forked polearm to capture criminals. Also: 刺股.

**141) 捻止 (sodegarami)**
Another man-catcher, with multiple barbs pointing forward and backwards. These prevents the person from grabbing it.

**Drawing #60**

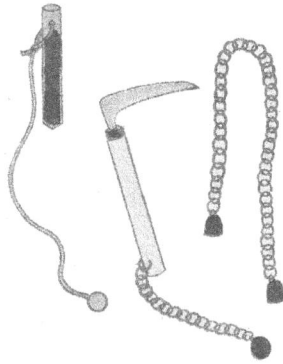

## 142) 鎖鎌 (*kusarigama*)
Middle; Chained sickle.

## 143) 鐵鎖 (*kusari*)
Metal chain with weights on both ends.

## 144) 懷棒 (*kaibo*)
Information not found.
But from the picture, it appears to be a flail weapon with rope, rather than metal chains.

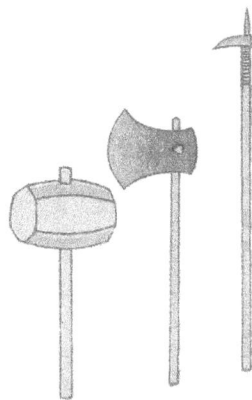

**Drawing #61**

---

## 145) 鳶嘴 (*tobiguchi*)
Right; Literally "Kite's Mouth", a fire-fighting tool with a side-hook.

## 146) 鉞 (*masakari*)
Middle; A battle axe.

## 147) 塭槌 (*otsuchi*)
Info not found. Nearest is "*otsuchi*", which is the Japanese war mallet.

**Drawing #62**

## 148) 打根 (*uchine*)
Right; Also "*uchiya*". Hand-thrown arrow.

## 149) 手裏劔 (*shuriken*)
Flying darts.

**Drawing #63**

## 150) 蒺藜 (*hishi*)
Bottom; Also "*makibishi*", which are spiked objects laid down on the ground.

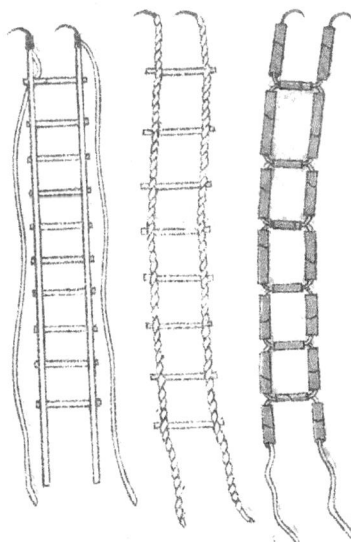

---

## 151) 管階子 (*kuda bashigo*)
Right; Literally "Tube Ladder". Notice that the ladder is made by passing ropes through multiple tubes.

## 152) 繩梯 (*nawa bashigo*)
Middle; A simple rope ladder.

## 153) 岩石階子 (*ganseki bashigo*)
Left; Literally "Rock Ladder". Notice that the ladder is rigid, but with ropes hanging down on both sides.

**Drawing #64**

# Page 9: Administrative Equipment

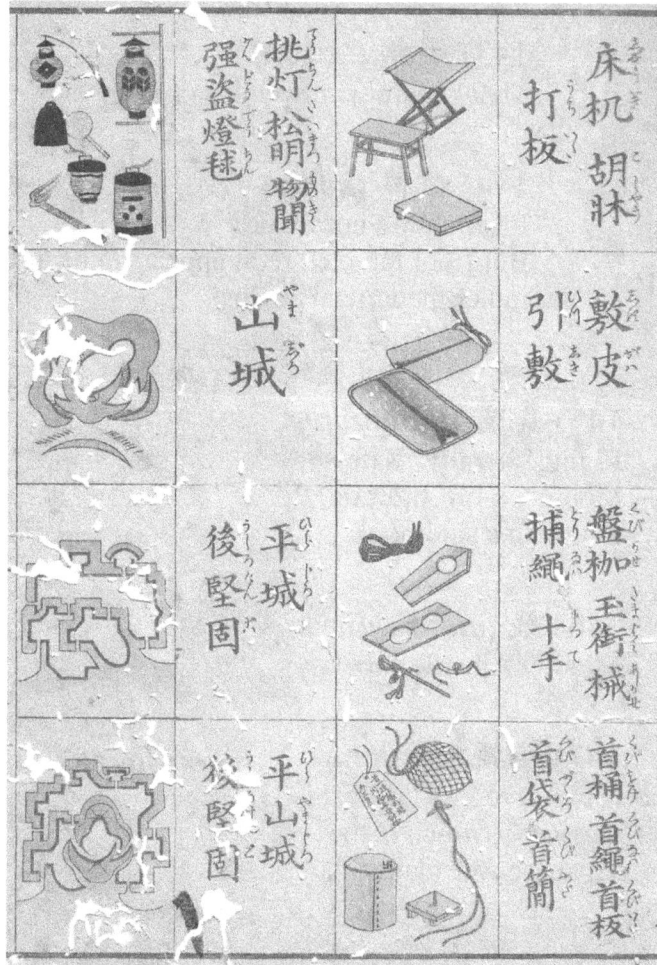

**Page 9 of the Drawings**

**Drawing #65**

154) 床机 (*shougi*)
Top; Military folding stool.

155) 胡牀 (*koshou*)
Middle; Rigid bench.

156) 打板 (*uchiita*)
Bottom; Literally "Striking Board".

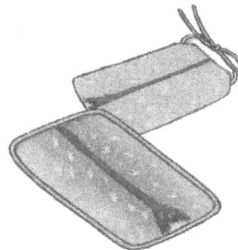

**Drawing #66**

157) 敷皮 (*shikigawa*)
Fur cushion.

158) 引敷 (*hikishiki*)
Seat apron, made of animal skin.

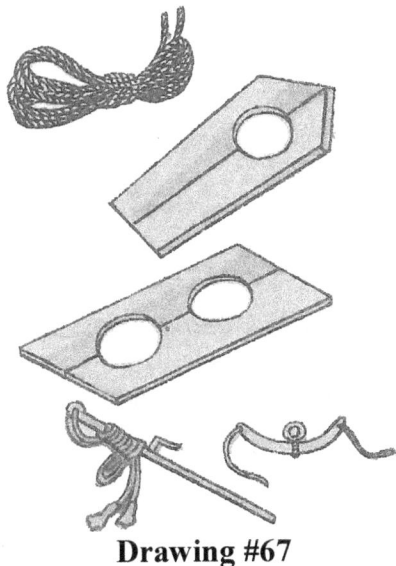
**Drawing #67**

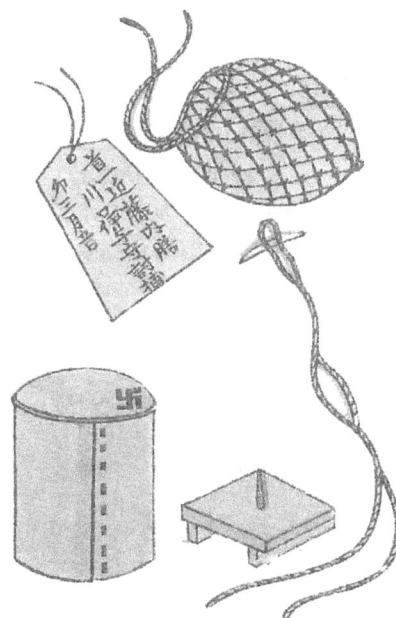
**Drawing #68**

### 159) 盤枷 (*kubikase*)

Middle; Wooden planks with holes. Criminals will have their heads and hands placed through them to shackle and restrain them.

### 160) 玉銜械 (*tamabukukase*)

Bottom-right; A mouth-gag made of jade.

### 161) 捕繩 (*torinawa*)

Top-left; Rope for tying criminals.

### 162) 十手 (*jitte*)

Bottom-left; Truncheon with a side-hook to lock and disarm the enemy's weapon.

---

### 163) 首桶 (*kubioke*)

Bottom-left; Literally "Head Bucket". Notice the religious symbol printed on the bucket.

### 164) 首繩 (*kubinawa*)

Right; Literally "Head Rope".

### 165) 首板 (*kubi ita*)

Bottom-right; Literally "Head Tray". Notice the spike in the middle, to ensure the head doesn't roll off the board.

### 166) 首袋 (*kubi bukuro*)

Top-right; Literally "Head Bag".

### 167) 首簡 (*kubi fuda*)

Top-left; Literally "Head Tag". The word 簡 indicates that this is made of bamboo. This is attached to the head for identification purpose.

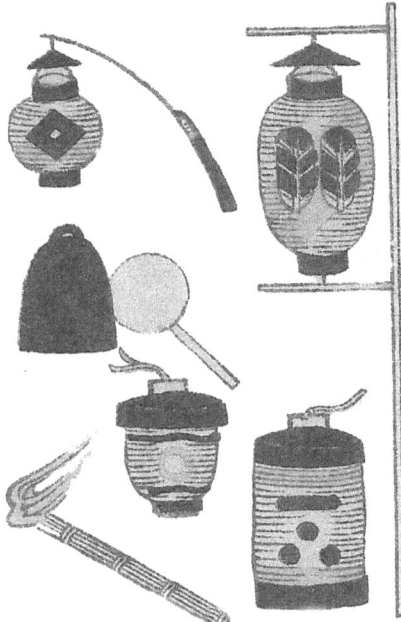

**Drawing #69**

## 168) 挑灯 (*chouchin*)
Right; Street lantern.

## 169) 松明 (*taimatsu*)
Bottom-left; Fire torch.

## 170) 物聞 (*monokiki*)
Middle-left; Literally "Sound Object". No information found. Best guess is, this is a small (black) bell, which you strike to make a sound. In Chinese history, a town will hire a person to walk around the streets at night, sounding off this bell, and announcing the time every now and then.

## 171) 強盗燈毬 (*boudou douchin*)
Literally "Bandit Light Ball". A lantern shaped like a ball, supposedly to keep out robbers.

---

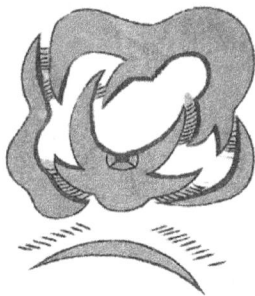

**Drawing #70**

## 172) 山城 (*yamajiro*)
Literally "Mountain Castle".

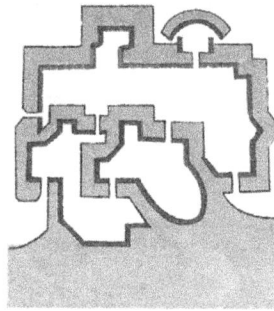

**Drawing #71**

## 173) 平城 後堅固 (*hirajiro – ushiro kengo*)
Castle build on flat plains, the rear is backed by something stiff and strong, possibly the base of a cliff.

---

**Drawing #72**

## 174) 平山城 後堅固 (*hirayamajiro – ushiro kengo*)
Castle built on the mountains. The rear is similarly backed by something stiff and strong, like a cliff.

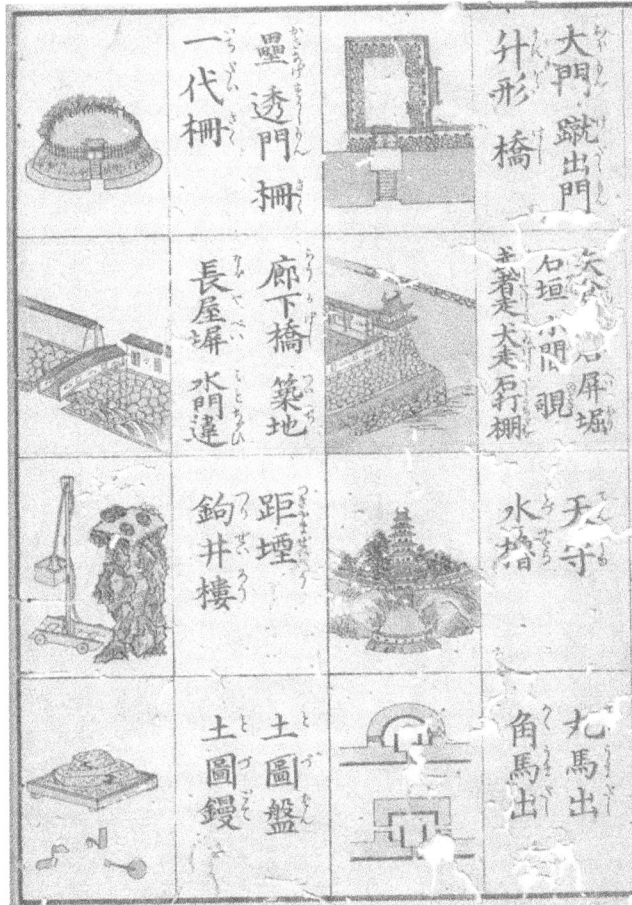

**Page 10 of the Drawings**

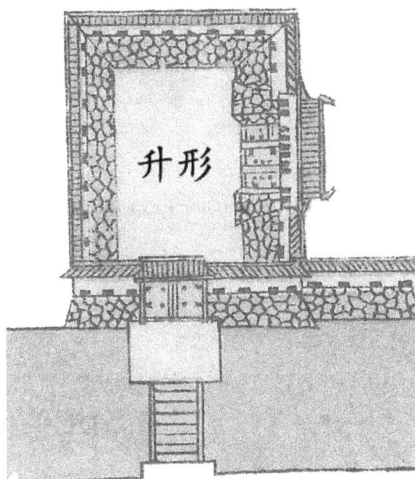

**Drawing #73**

## 175) 大門 (*oomon*)
Large front gate (facing towards the right).

## 176) 蹴出門 (*kedashimon*)
The door facing the bridge (bottom).

## 177) 升形 (*masugata*)
A gathering space for troops, between the inner & outer gates.

## 178) 橋 (*hashi*)
Bridge.

**Drawing #74**

**179) 矢倉 (*yagura*)**
Watch tower.

**180) 屏掘 (*heibori*)**
Walled moat.

**181) 石垣 (*ishigaki*)**
Stone wall.

**182) 小間 (*koma*)**
Small room.

**183) 覗 (*nozoki*)**
Small holes in the walls for peeping.

**184) 武者走 (*musha bashiri*)**
Walking paths inside the castle.

**185) 犬走 (*inu bashiri*)**
"Dog's Path". Notice between the base of the stone walls, and the green grass, there is a very narrow dirt path.

**186) 石打棚 (*ishiuchibana*)**
Notice behind the castle walls, there are wooden platforms erected. Soldiers can stand here to throw rocks.

**Drawing #75**

## 187) 天守 (*tenshu*)
Literally "Sky Defence". This is a castle tower.

## 188) 水櫓 (*mizuyagura*)
This is for the purpose of drawing water into the castle, for the residents to use.

---

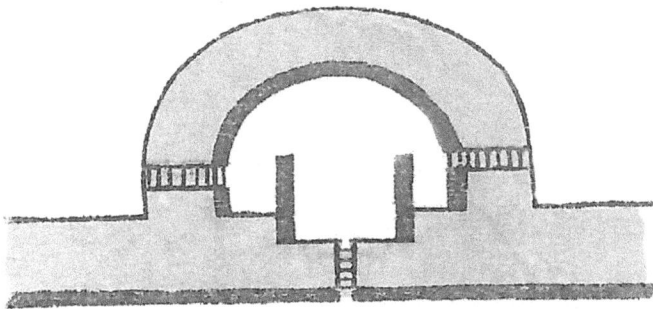

## 189) 丸馬出
(*maru umadashi*)
Top; Staging area for troops. Rounded design.

## 190) 角馬出
(*kaku umadashi*)
Below; Same, but square-ish design.

Troops form up at this staging area first, then exit via the left/right. This provides a tactical advantage.

3. Enemy forces are outside here.

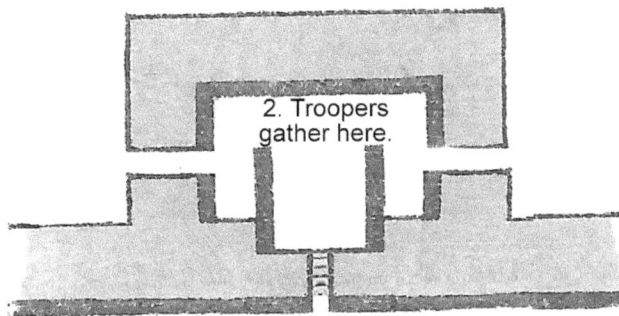

2. Troopers gather here.

1. Allied forces reside here in the castle.

**Drawing #76**

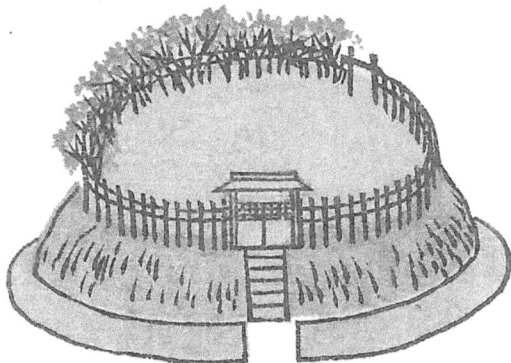
**Drawing #77**

### 191) 塁 (*kasa-age*)
A small building/castle that is built on piled up soil and rocks.

### 192) 透門 (*sukashimon*)
A type of castle door which has a beam above.

### 193) 柵 (*saku*) Fence or railing.

### 194) 一代柵 (*ichidai saku*)
Likely referring to a single layer of railings.

**Drawing #78**

### 195) 廊下橋 (*roukabashi*)
A bridge which has a roof constructed for greater safety.

### 196) 築地 (*tsuiji*)
Left; Mud wall constructed with a roof.

### 197) 長屋塀 (*nagaya bei*)
Right; Long wall fence.

### 198) 水門違 (*mito chigai*)
Notice that the waterway below the bridge is narrower. This is to create a blockade and prevent boats from being able to travel all the way around the castle.
"*chigai*" means "different". The moats are compartmentalized by different heights, so that the water from one segment doesn't mix with the other.

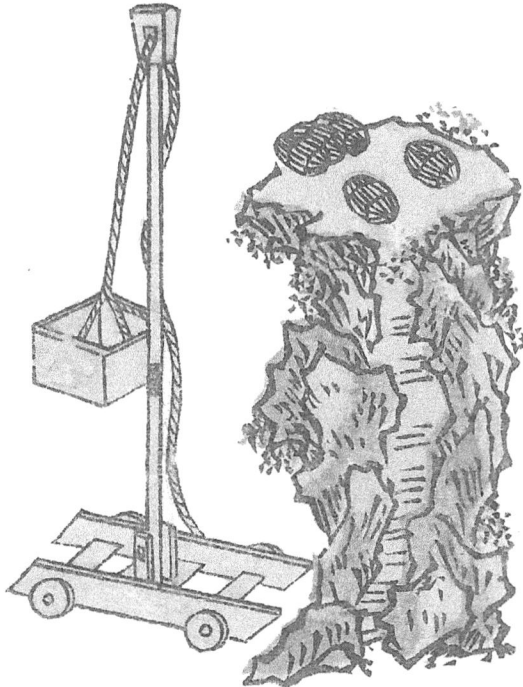

**Drawing #79**

199) 距堙
**(*tsukiyama*)**
Right; Literally "Hill Garden". According to the Chinese classic "Sun Tzu Art of War", this is a man-made soil hill built near the enemy castle, for the purpose of observation and/or invasion.

200) 鉤井樓
**(*harizerou*)**
Watch-tower. Notice that the platform can be pulled up by the ropes, almost like an elevator.

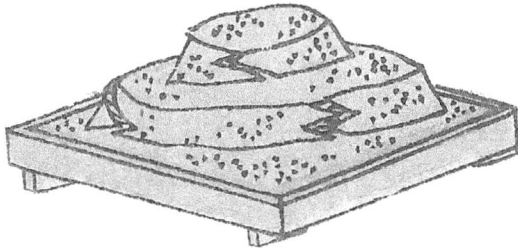

201) 土圖盤
**(*tozuban*)**
Top; Soil board.

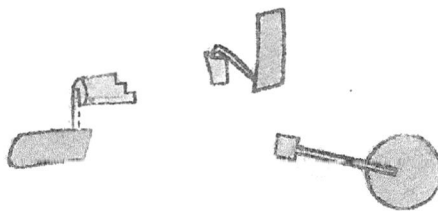

202) 土圖鏝
**(*tsuiji*)**
Bottom; Soil trowel.

**Drawing #80**

# Page 11: Encampment Equipment

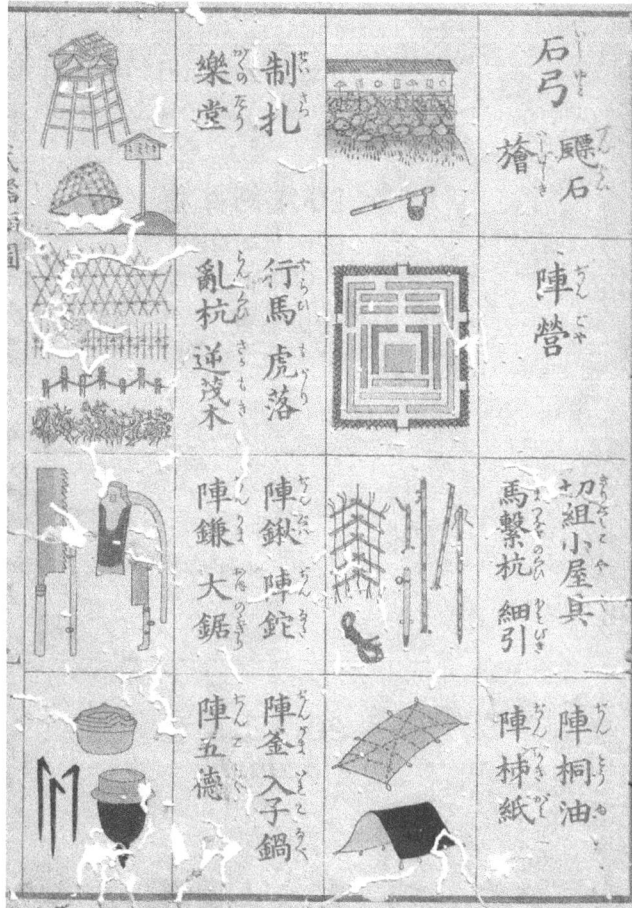

**Page 11 of the Drawings**

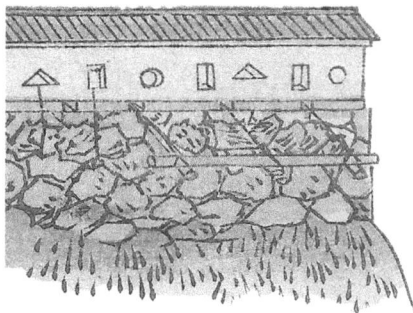

### 203) 石弓 (*ishiyumi*)

Literally "Rock Bow". Notice that rocks are hung on the wall's right-side. These can be released and dropped down onto the enemies below.

### 204) 颿石 (*zunbai*)

Bottom; Used like an atlatl. Rocks are placed in the small basket and thrown.

**Drawing #81**

### 205) 簹 (*ishibashiki*)

Info not found. Best guess: These are the holes in the walls for soldiers to throw rocks.

**Drawing #82**

## 206) 陣営
**(*jingoya*)**
Military encampment.
Notice the camp is surrounded by fences.

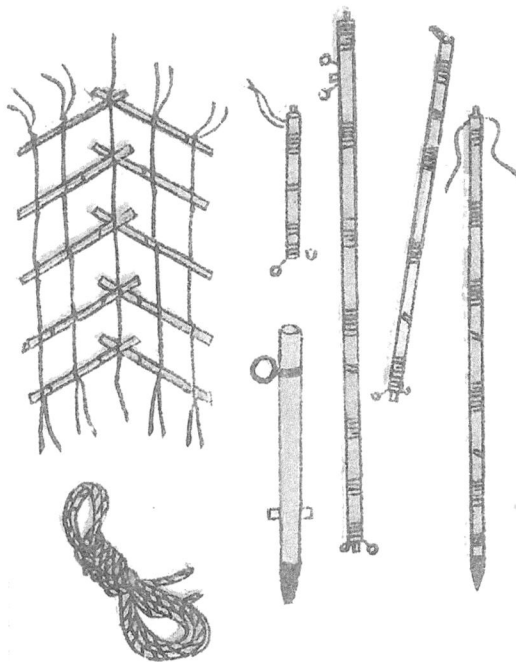

**Drawing #83**

## 207) 切組小屋具
**(*kirigumi koyagu*)**
Pieces to pitch a shed for troops to stay.

## 208) 馬繋杭
**(*umatsunagi no kui*)**
Middle; A stake for securing the horse to.
It has ring at the top for ropes to pass
through.

## 209) 細引
**(*hosobiki*)**
Bottom-right; Hempen cord or rope.

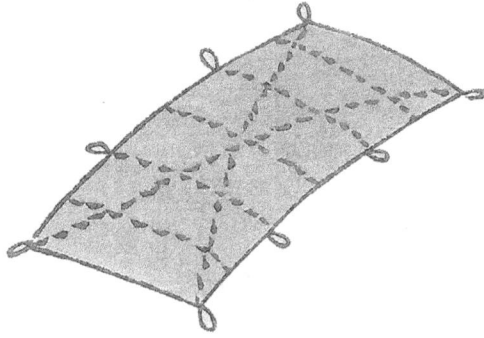

## 210) 陣桐油 (*jintouyu*)

This is paper smeared with 桐油, "tung oil", which makes it waterproof. Useful in the setting up of troops' encampment.

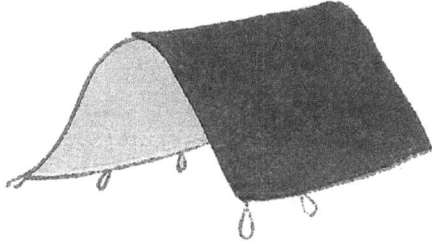

## 211) 陣柿紙 (*jinkakigami*)

Paper treated with persimmon juice (*kakishibu*). The long treatment process turns the paper into a deep brown color, and becomes waterproof, strong and extremely durable.

**Drawing #84**

## 212) 制扎 (*seisatsu*)

Bottom-right; A wooden post with words written on it. Like a signpost or notice board.

## 213) 楽堂 (*raku no dou*)

A place for troops to chill and relax.
Top is the elevated version.
Bottom is the grounded version.

**Drawing #85**

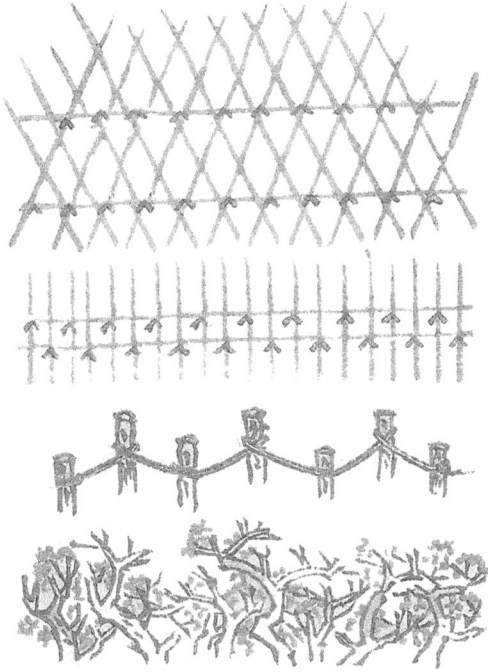
**Drawing #86**

**214) 行馬 (*yarai*)**
Top; Bamboo fence. Read also: 矢来.

**215) 虎落 (*mogari*)**
2nd from Top; Bamboo fence. Vertical design.

**216) 亂杭 (*rangui*)**
3rd from top; Wooden stakes planted into the ground as a defensive barrier.

**217) 逆茂木 (*sakamogi*)**
Bottom; Thorny branches facing outwards, also as a defensive barrier.

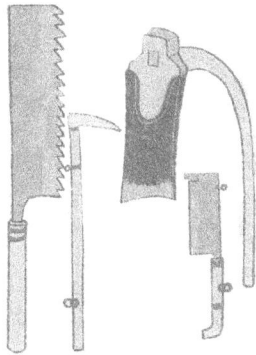
**Drawing #87**

**218) 陣鍬 (*jin guwa*)**
Military hoe.

**219) 陣鉈 (*jin nata*)**
Military hatchet.

**220) 陣鎌 (*jin kama*)**
Military sickle.

**221) 大鋸 (*ooga*)**
Large saw. In the book, the Hiragana reads as "*oo no togari*".

**Drawing #88**

**222) 陣釜 (*jin gama*)**
Military pot/kettle.

**223) 入子鍋 (*ireko nabe*)**
Top; Pots which has smaller versions, so that they can be stacked together.

**224) 陣五德 (*jin gotoku*)**
Left; Tripod meant as a kettle-stand. You will stab each piece into the ground, and the pot will rest on the small horizontal parts.

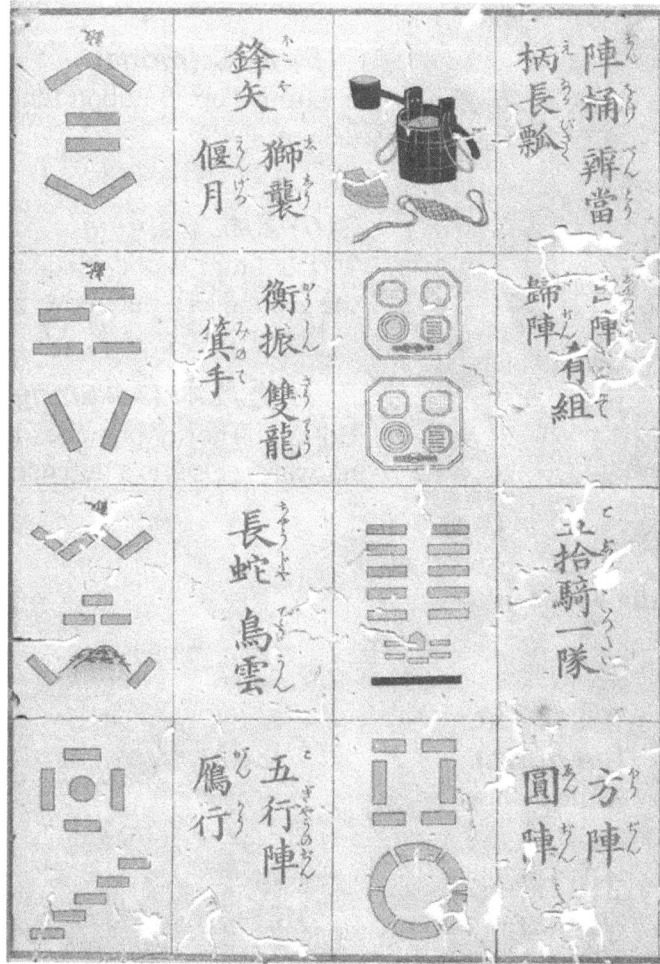

**Page 12 of the Drawings**

**Drawing #89**

225) 陣桶
(*jin oke*)
Military bucket.

226) 辨當
(*bento*)
Left; Meal box.

227) 柄長瓢
(*enaga bisako*)
Dried gourd used as a flask or water bottle.

打鮑
*uchi-awabi*

Few slices
of Abalone

勝栗
*kachiguri*

"Victory"
Chestnuts

昆布
*kombu*

Kelp

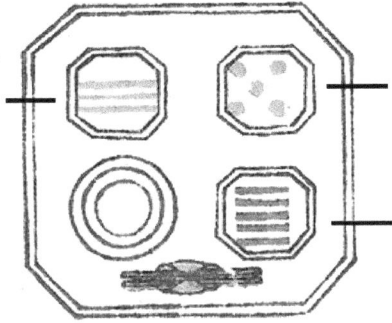

228)
出陣
(**shutsujin**) = Departing for war.

帰陣 (**kijin**) = Returning from war.

肴組 (**sakana gumi**) = Appetizer meal.

These 2 drawings show a good-luck meal treat for those departing for and returning from war.

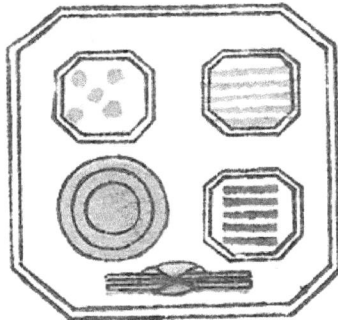

**Drawing #90**

---

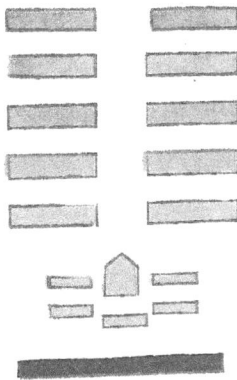

**Drawing #91**

229) 五拾騎一隊
(**gojuki itai**)
50 horseback
Samurai as 1 cavalry
company.

Note that 拾 is the
same as 十, which
means 10.

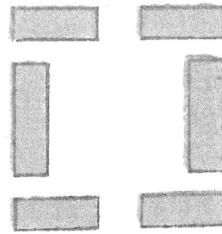

230) 方陣
(**houjin**)
Square battle
formation.

231) 圓陣
(**enjin**)
Rounded battle
formation.

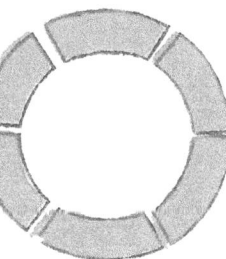

**Drawing #92**

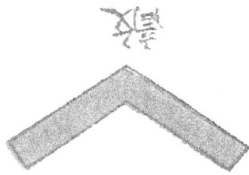

232) 鋒矢
(*hokoya*)
Formation shaped like the tip of an arrow.

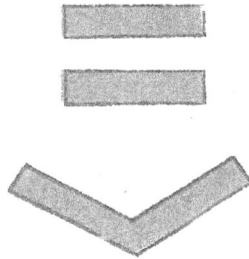

233) 獅襲
(*shishuu*)
Literally "Lion Attack" formation.

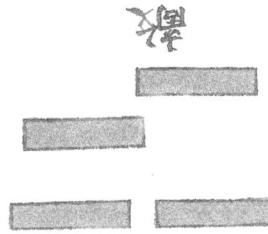

234) 偃月
(*engetsu*)
Literally "Crescent" formation.

**Drawing #93**

235) 衡振
(*koushin*)
A horizontal battle formation.

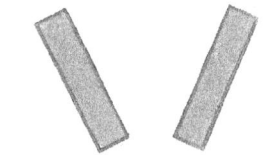

236) 雙龍
(*souryuu*)
Literally "Double Dragon" formation.

237) 箕手
(*minote*)
Literally "Winnower" formation.

**Drawing #94**

238) 長蛇
(*chouja*)
Literally "Long Snake" formation.

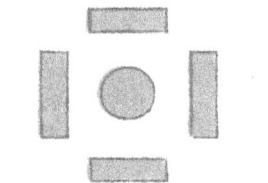

239) 鳥雲
(*chou un*)
Literally "Bird Cloud" formation. Notice that the troops are lined up at the base of a mountain.

**Drawing #95**

240) 五行陣
(*gogyou no jin*)
Top; The "5 Elements" Formation.

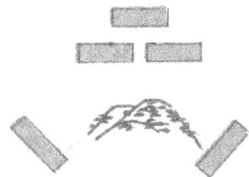

241) 鴈行
(*gankou*)
Bottom; The "Wild Goose" Formation.

**Drawing #96**

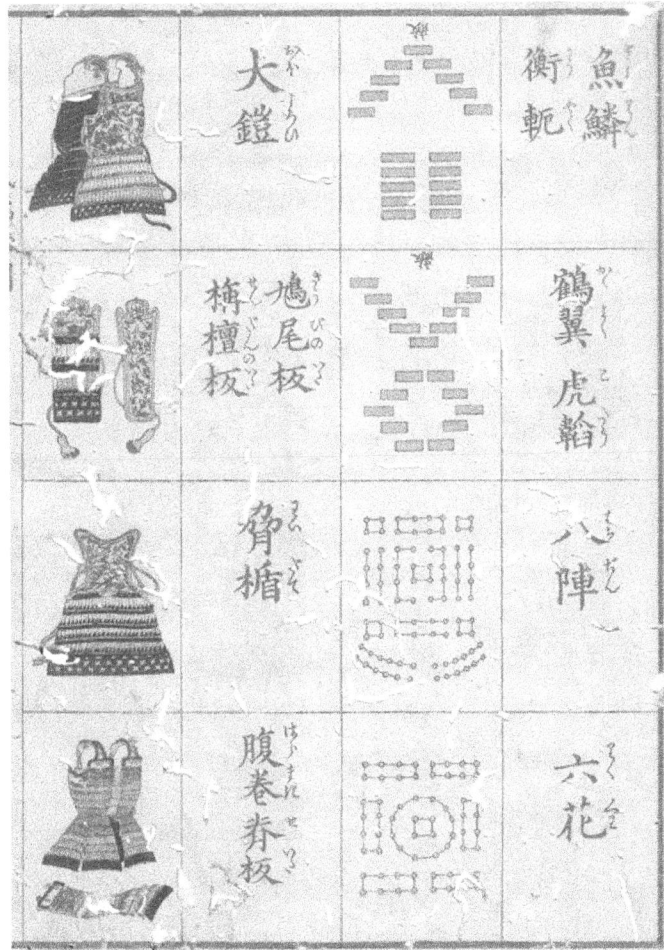

**Page 13 of the Drawings**

**Drawing #97**

242) 魚鱗 **(gyorin)**
Top; Literally "Fish Scales" formation.

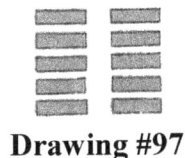

243) 衡軛 **(kouyaku)**
Bottom; A formation organized in a neat and balanced way.

**Drawing #98**

244) 鶴翼 **(kakuyoku)**
Top; Literally "Crane's Wings" formation, resembling a crane spreading its wings.

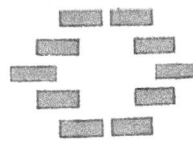

245) 虎韜 **(koutou)**
Bottom; Also written as 虎頭, which means "Tiger's Head".

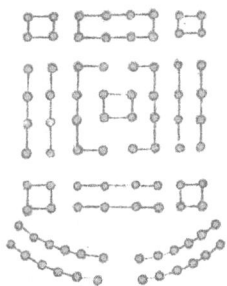

**246) 八陣 (hachijin)**
Literally "8 Battle Formations".

**Drawing #99**

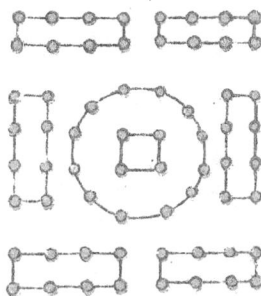

**247) 六花 (rokka)**
Literally "Six Flowers" formation.
.

**Drawing #100**

**Drawing #101**

**248) 大鎧 (oo yoroi)**
Literally "Big Armour". Big boxy shaped armour designed for cavalry Archers.

**Drawing #102**

**249) 鳩尾板 (kyuubi no ita)**
Right; This piece is attached to the left shoulder, and hung down over the left chest.

**250) 栴檀板 (sendan no ita)**
Left; This piece is attached to the right shoulder, and hung down over the right chest.

**Drawing #103**

**251) 脅楯 (waidate)**
Protective plate for the right flank.

**Drawing #104**

**252) 腹巻 (haramaki)**
This type of armour is literally named as "Stomach Wrap".

**253) 背板 (se ita)**
Because the 'Haramaki' style of armour leaves the wearer's spine exposed, this piece is subsequently worn to provide protection there.

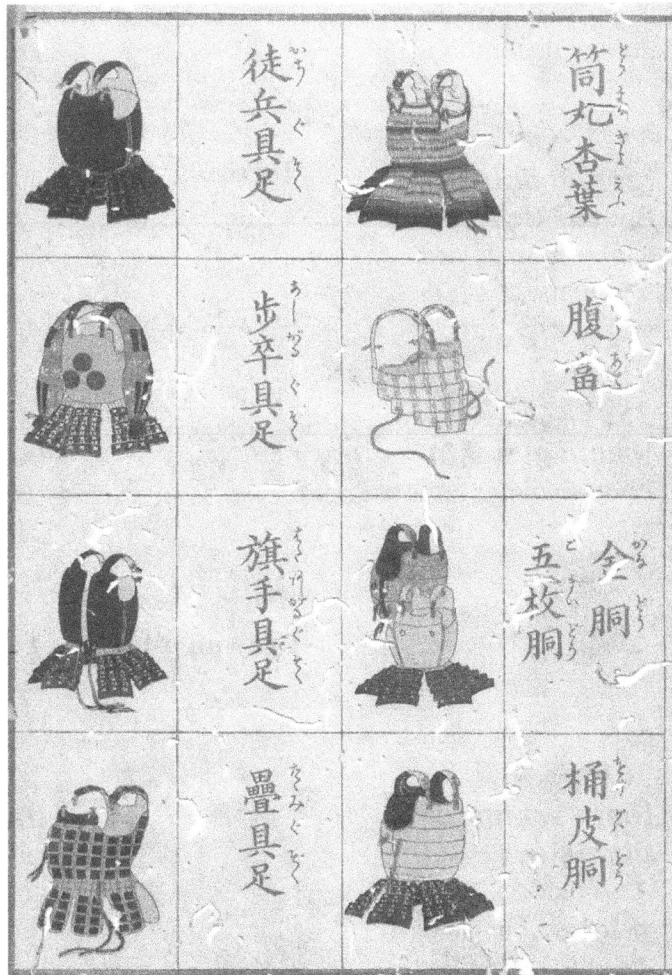

**Page 14 of the Drawings**

## 254) 筒丸杏葉
### (*doumaru kyouyou*)
The '*Domaru*' style of armour.

**Drawing #105**

## 255) 腹當
### (*hara ate*)
The '*Hara-ate*' style is a more economical and simpler type of armour, which protects only the front of the wearer.

**Drawing #106**

**256) 金胴
(kanedou)**
Top; Body armour with
golden decorations.

**257) 五枚胴
(gomai dou)**
Bottom; Body armour
which is made of 5
segments.

**Drawing #107**

**258) 桶皮胴
(okegawa dou)**
Body armour shaped like
a tub.

**Drawing #108**

**259) 徒兵具足
(kachi gusoku)**
Foot-soldier's armour.

**Drawing #109**

**260) 歩卒具足
(ashigaru gusoku)**
Armour worn by the
'Ashigaru' soldiers.

**Drawing #110**

**261) 旗手具足
(hata ashigaru
gusoku)**
Also read as "kishu
gusoku". This is the
armour for the flag-
carriers.

**Drawing #111**

**262) 畳具足
(tatami gusoku)**
Lightweight and foldable
armour, made with
multiple rectangular
pieces.

**Drawing #112**

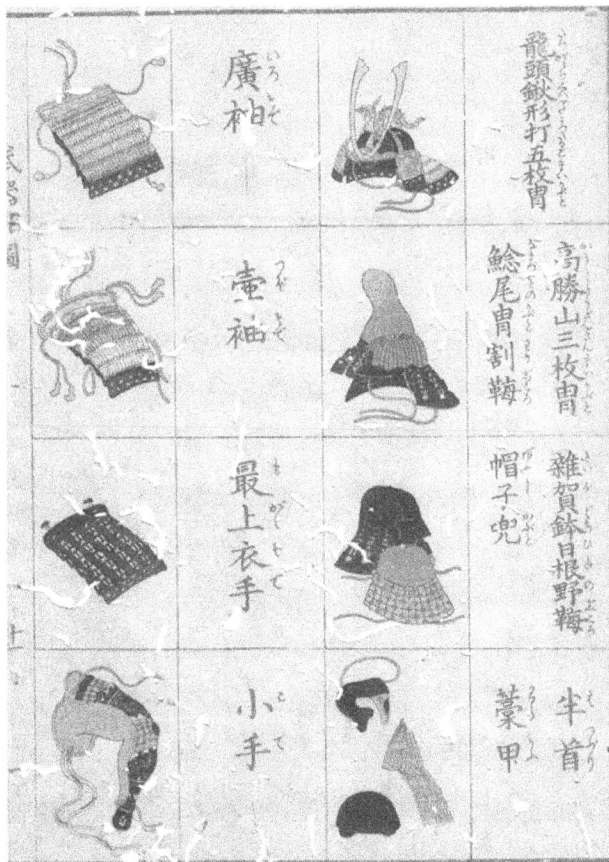

**Page 15 of the Drawings**

**Drawing #113**

263)
**龍頭鍬形打五枚胃**
**(*ryuugashira kuwagata utsugomai kabuto*)**
An elaborate helmet with a dragon on top. 5 plate design.

**Drawing #114**

264) **高勝山三枚胃**
**(*koushouzan sanmai kabuto*)**
Front; The "High Victory Mountain" helmet. 3 plate design.

265) **鯰尾胃割革毎**
**(*namazuo no kabuto wari-jikoro*)**
Behind; "Catfish's Tail" Helmet. With a split nape guard (*shikoro*).

**Drawing #115**

266)
雑賀鉢日根野革毎
(*saiga hineno jikoro*)
Behind; The "*hineno*" style helmet.

267) 帽子兜
(*boshi kabuto*)
Hat-shaped Helmet.

**Drawing #116**

268) 半首
(*hatsuburi*)
Top; Half-face armour.

269) 薫甲
(*warakou*)
Straw gear.

---

**Drawing #117**

270) 廣袖
(*hiro sode*)
Literally "Wide Sleeve".
Shoulder armour.

**Drawing #118**

271) 壷袖
(*tsubo sode*)
Literally "Jar Sleeve".
This shoulder armour has curved plates, so that it 'wraps' around the wearer's arm.

---

**Drawing #119**

272) 最上衣手
(*mogami sode*)
Literally "Best Sleeve". This shoulder armour was more compact, and usually attached together with a "*mogami*" style set of armour.

**Drawing #120**

273) 小手
(*kote*)
As seen, this is the armour for the arm and hand.

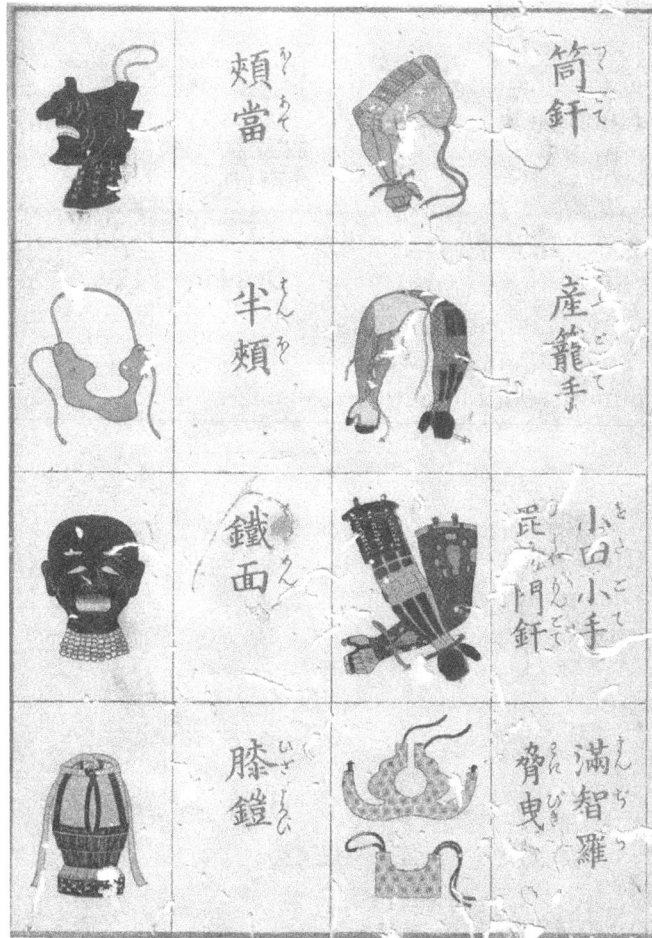

**Page 16 of the Drawings**

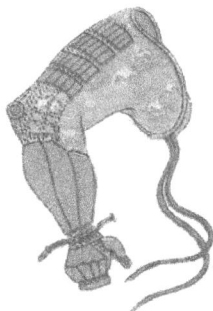

## 274) 筒鈝
**(*tsutsu gote*)**

This design covered the entire arm with mail, while the upper-arm and forearm are further protected with plates.

**Drawing #121**

## 275) 産籠手
**(*ubu gote*)**

In this design, the protective plates arc sandwiched and sewn inside the fabric.

Notice also it's a 1-piece design for both arms.

**Drawing #122**

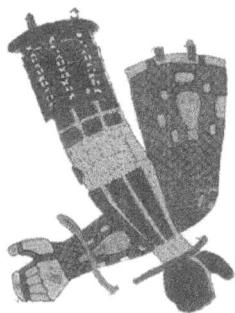

**276) 小田小手
(oda gote)**
Right; These are identified by the gourd-shaped plates found on the upper arm and forearm.

**Drawing #123**

**277) 毘沙門釬
(bishamon gote)**
Left; This design has a "*sode*", shoulder armour, built into it.

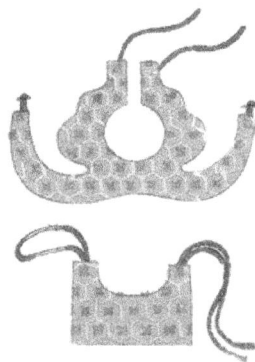

**278) 満智羅
(manchira)**
Top; This is a "*kikko manchira*" armour, made with small hexagon plates.

**Drawing #124**

**279) 脅曳
(wakibiki)**
Bottom; Similar "*kikko*" design, made with small hexagon plates. This is armour for the arm-pit.

**280) 頬當
(hou ate)**
Face protector, with a hanging neck guard.

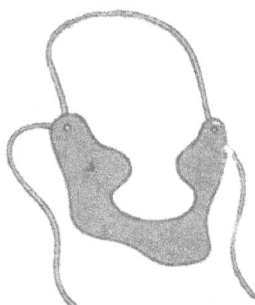

**Drawing #125**

**281) 半頬
(han hou)**
Half-face protector.

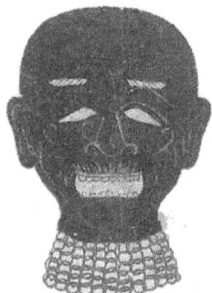

**Drawing #126**

**282) 鐵面
(tetsu men)**
Literally "Metal Face". Full face protector. Notice the hanging chainmail to protect the neck.

**Drawing #127**

**283) 膝鎧
(hiza yoroi)**
Literally "Knee Armour".

**Drawing #128**

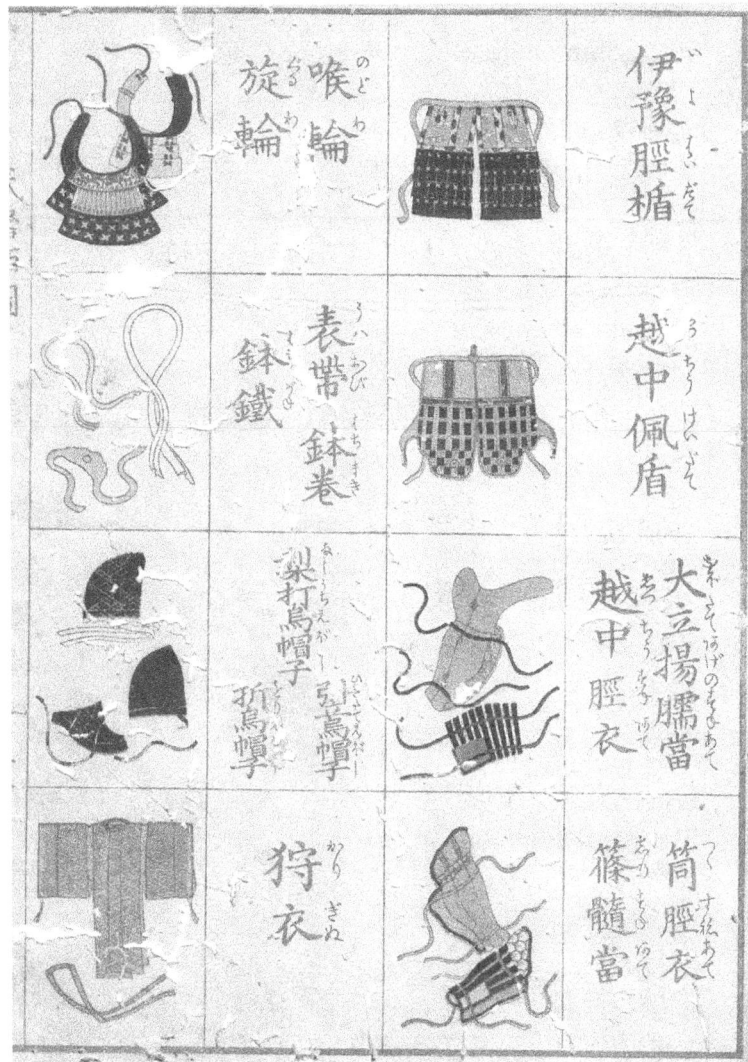

**Page 17 of the Drawings**

**Drawing #129**

284) 伊豫脛楯
(*iyo haidate*)
Thigh armour, from
"*Iyo no Kuni*", south-
western part of Japan.

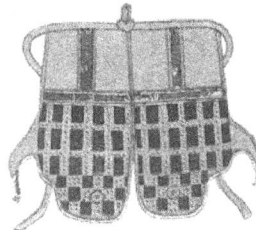

**Drawing #130**

285) 越中佩盾
(*ecchu haidate*)
Thigh armour, from
"*Ecchu no Kuni*", middle
part of Japan.
Notice that the Kanji for
"*haidate*" is different.

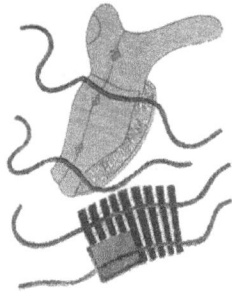
**Drawing #131**

286) 大立揚臑當 (**ootateage no suneate**)
Top; Shin guard, with extra protection spilling upwards onto the knee/thigh area.

287) 越中脛衣 (**ecchu suneate**)
Shin guard from "*Ecchu no Kuni*".

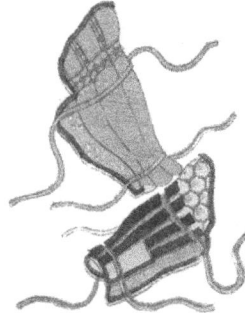
**Drawing #132**

288) 筒脛衣 (**tsutsu suneate**)
Top; 3-plated shin guard.

289) 篠髓當 (**shino suneate**)
Bottom; Bamboo shin guard.

---

**Drawing #133**

290) 喉輪 (**nodawa**)
Throat protector. The ropes for this are tied together behind the neck.

291) 旋輪 (**guruwa**)
Wrapped completely around the neck.

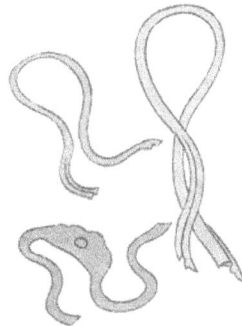
**Drawing #134**

292) 表帶 (**uwa obi**)
Front belt.

293) 鉢帶 (**hachi obi**)
Forehead band.

294) 鉢鐵 (**hachigane**)
Bottom; Metal forehead protector.

---

**Drawing #135**

295) 梨打鳥帽子 (**nashiuchi eboshi**)
Soft hat, which can be worn under a helmet.

296) 引立鳥帽子 (**hikitate eboshi**)
Soft hat, with white straps to tie it securely around the wearer's head.

297) 折鳥帽子 (**ori eboshi**)
Bottom; Folded '*eboshi*'.

**Drawing #136**

298) 狩衣 (**kariginu**)
Casual wear for the nobles.

**Page 18 of the Drawings**

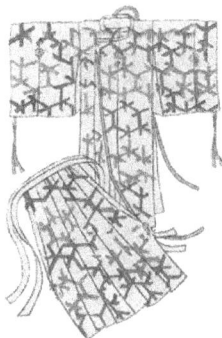

**299) 水干**
**(*suikan*)**
Daily wear, worn by nobles, in ancient Japan.

**Drawing #137**

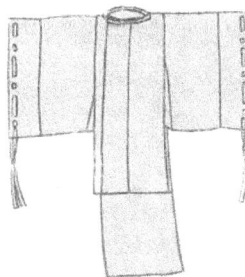

**300) 淨衣**
**(*jyou e*)**
White robe, usually worn at religious events.

**Drawing #138**

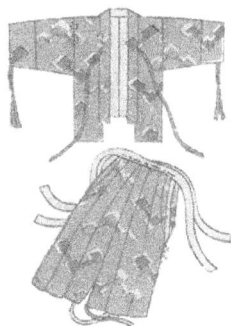

**301) 鎧直垂**
**(yoroi hitatare)**
Top and bottom worn underneath the armour.

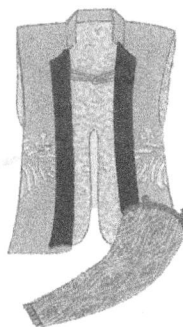

**Drawing #139**

**302) 弓鞢**
**(yugote)**
Single sleeve worn by Archers.

**303) 陣羽織**
**(jin baori)**
Battle surcoat.

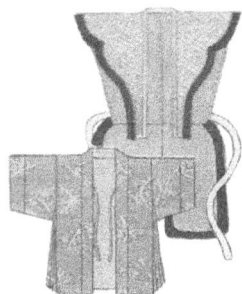

**Drawing #140**

**304) 胴肩衣**
**(dou kataginu)**
A sleeveless version of "dou fuku".

**Drawing #141**

**305) 胴服**
**(dou fuku)**
A jacket worn by high-ranking Samurai, over their clothing or armour.

**306) 鎧襯**
**(yoroi hadagi)**
Shirt worn by lower-ranking warriors, underneath their armour.

**Drawing #142**

**307) 聯索肌著**
**(renzaku hadagi)**
Top; Chainmail version of "hadagi".

**308) 犢鼻褌**
**(tafu sagi)**
Bottom; Loincloth, traditional Japanese male underwear.

**309) 大口袴**
**(ooguchi no hakama)**
Literally "Big Hole Hakama". Usually worn as an undergarment.

**310) 四幅襠**
**(yonobakama)**
Knee-length Hakama, with 2 panels in front and 2 panels behind.

**Drawing #143**

**311) 小袴**
**(kobakama)**
Literally "Small Hakama", usually worn by lower-class warriors.

**Drawing #144**

**Page 19 of the Drawings**

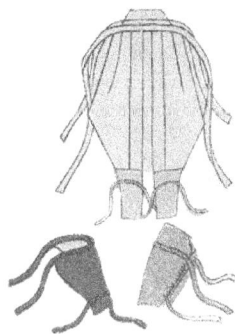

**Drawing #145**

**Drawing #146**

312) 革袴
**(*kuwa bakama*)**
Leather version of the *Hakama*.

313) 脛巾
**(*habaki*)**
Fabric leggings worn at the shin.

314) 裏甲 **(*kikomi*)**
Top; Chainmail armour.

315) 股引
**(*momohiki*)**
Traditional Japanese bottom, tends to be slim-fit.

316) 三尺手拭
**(*sanjyaku tenugui*)**
Bottom; A 3-*shaku* long hand towel.

317) 陣笠
(*jingasa*)
Soldier's head-wear.

318) 冑當
(*muneate*)
Left; An apron-like chest protector.

**Drawing #147**

319) 頭巾 (*zukin*)
Hood which covers the whole face except the eyes.

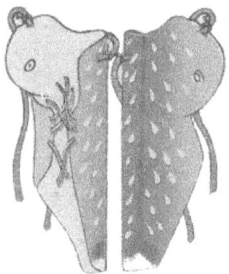

**Drawing #148**

320) 綾藺笠
(*ayaigasa*)
Top; Hat with a cone on top. Seen at Yabusame demonstration.

321) 竹笠
(*takegasa*)
Bottom; Bamboo hat.

322) 行縢
(*mukabaki*)
Deerskin worn on the legs. Commonly observed at *Yabusame* demonstrations.

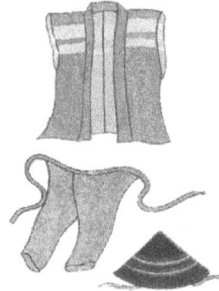

**Drawing #149**

**Drawing #150**

323) 小者半臂
(*komono hanbi*)
Sleeveless jacket worn by low-status servant.

324) 笠 (*kasa*)
Bottom; Hat.

325) 股曳 (*matahiki*)
Bottom-left; Traditional work trousers.

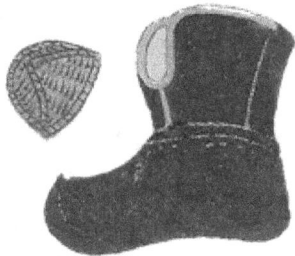

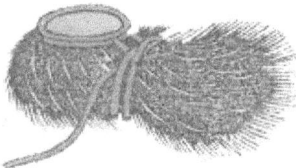

326) 煩貫
(*tsura nuki*)
Bottom; Footwear for walking on snow and ice.

327) 馬上沓
(*bajou gutsu*)
Top; Footwear meant for horse-riding.

328) 足半
(*ashinaka*)
Top-left; Straw sandals, only for the front portion of the foot.

**Drawing #151**

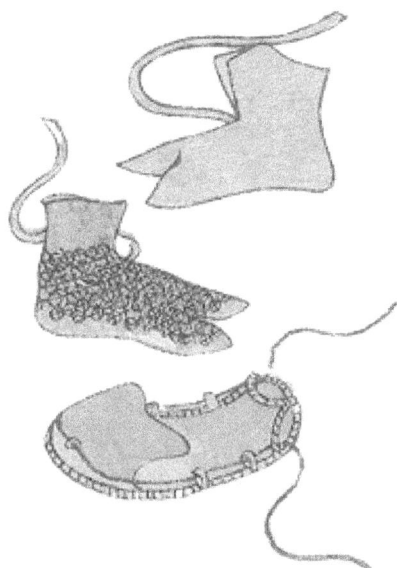

**Drawing #152**

## 329) 單皮 (*tabi*)
Top; Traditional socks.

## 330) 鏈足袋
(*kusari tabi*)
Middle; Chainmail socks.

## 331) 草鞋 (*waraji*)
Bottom; Straw sandals.

## 332) 鼻返 (*hanagaeshi*)
This is an extra flap, observed at the front of the straw sandals. It is folded backwards to cover the top of the toes.

# Page 20: Accessories

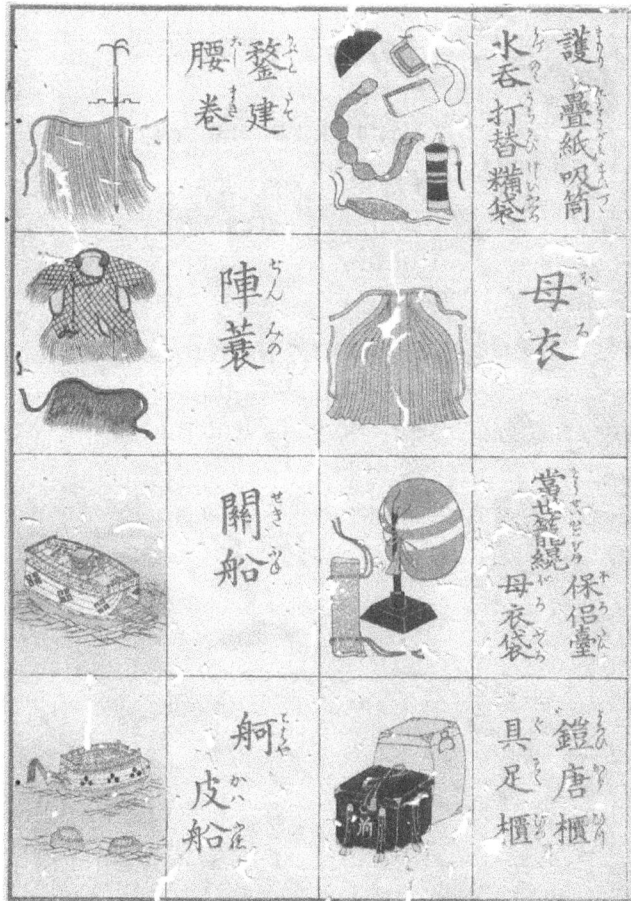

**Page 20 of the Drawings**

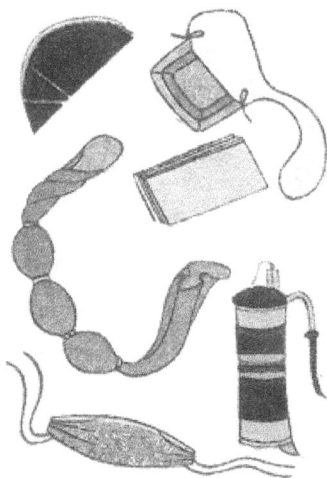

**Drawing #153**

**333) 護 (*mamori*)**
Amulet, lucky charm.

**334) 疊紙 (*tatougami*)**
Wrapping paper or folding paper case.

**335) 吸筒 (*suizutsu*)**
Straw.

**336) 水呑 (*mizunomi*)**
Drinking container.

**337) 打替 (*uchigae*)**
This should be written as 打ち飼ひ. A bag which you store your valuables in, then wrapped around your waist.

**338) 糒袋 (*hoshii bukuro*)**
Middle-left; Bag for storing dried boiled rice. This is then wrapped around the body. Each "lump" is one serving.

54

**339) 母衣 (horo)**
A cloth that covers your back, to protect you from arrows in battle.

**Drawing #154**

**340) 當世籠縲 (tousei kagoboro)**
Right; Similarly, a "horo" that's being used to protect your back from arrows. "Tousei" means the current version that is being used.

**Drawing #155**

**341) 保侶臺 (horodai)**
A stand for the "horo".

**342) 母衣袋 (horo bukuro)**
Bag for storing the "horo".

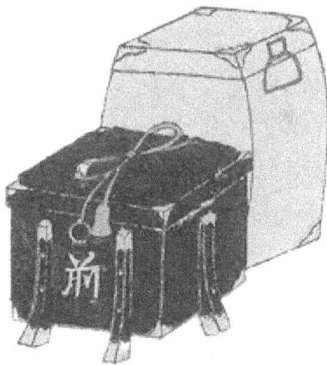

**343) 鎧唐櫃 (yoroi karabitsu)**
Left; A six-legged Chinese chest for storing armour.

Notice that the word 前 (mae) which means 'front', is written on it.

**Drawing #156**

**344) 具足櫃 (gusoku bitsu)**
Right; Also a chest for storing armour, but a more plain & simple design.

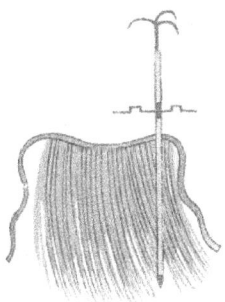

**345) 鍪建 (kabuto tate)**
A stand for displaying the helmet.

**346) 腰巻 (koshimaki)**
Literally "Waist Wrap". Ceremonial wear for Samurai women.

**Drawing #157**

**347) 陣簑 (jin mino)**
Straw coat and skirt.

**Drawing #158**

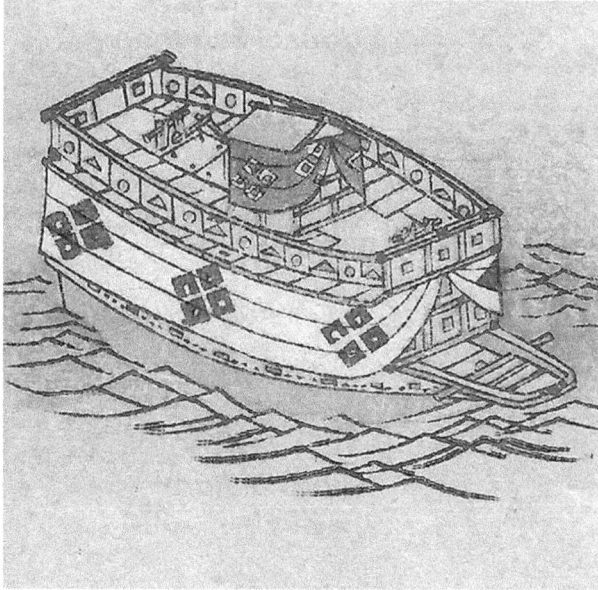
**Drawing #159**

## 348) 關船
### (sekifune)
A boat used for collecting fees from other boats who are passing by a certain path. It is built for speed, so that it can chase down boats that don't pay.

**Drawing #160**

## 349) 舸
### (hakafune)
A fast moving military ship.

## 350) 皮船
### (kawafune)
Bottom; Literally "Leather Boat". Small tub-shaped boat. Can only fit 1 or 2 persons.

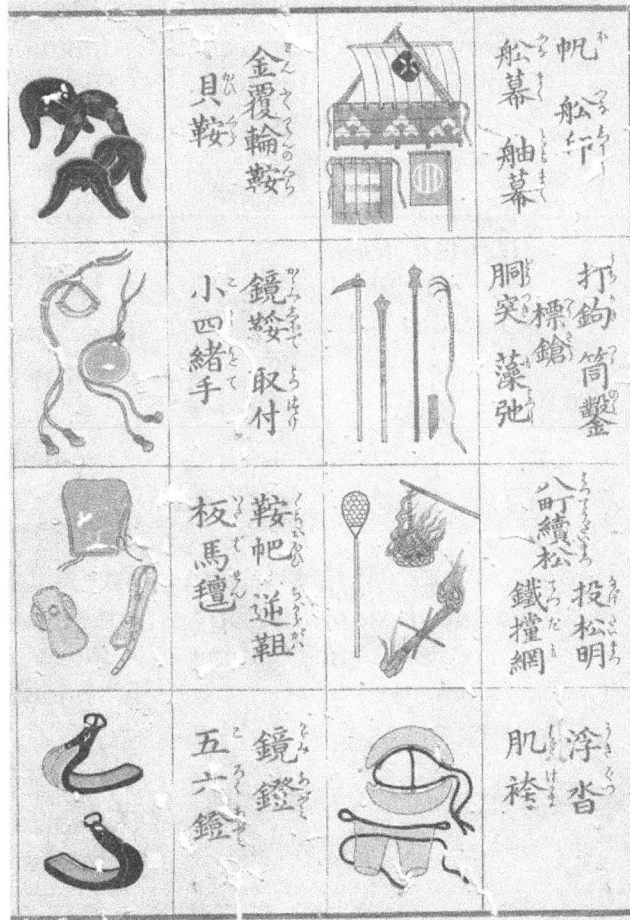

**Page 21 of the Drawings**

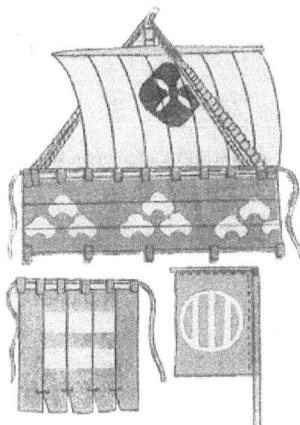

**Drawing #161**

351) 帆
(*ho*)
Top; Sail.

352) 舩印
(*fune shirushi*)
Flag with crest for a ship.

353) 舩幕
(*fune maku*)
Boat curtain.

354) 舳幕
(*fune maku*)
Curtain for the bow of a ship.

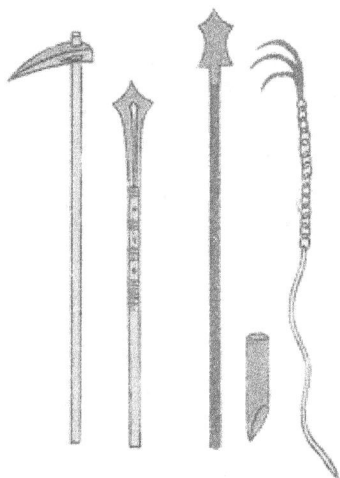

**Drawing #162**

355) 打鉤
(*uchikagi*)
Right; A hook which you can throw at a ledge, then climb up the rope. Or, for boats, you can pull them nearer.

356) 筒鑿
(*tsutsu nomi*)
Second-right, Bottom; Tube shaped chisel.

357) 標鎗 (*hyousou*)
Middle; Javelin. This is the same as found in Chinese military manuals, which depicts Shield fighters throwing these.

358) 胴突 (*dou tsuki*)
Second-left; A ramming tool/weapon.

359) 藻弛 (*motayu*)
As observed, it a pole weapon with a sideways pointed end.

**Drawing #163**

360) 八町續松
(*hacchou daimatsu*)
Top; A hanging burning torch.

361) 投松明
(*nage taimatsu*)
A throwing torch. Notice it's burning on both ends,

362) 鐵撞網
(*tetsudamo*)
Left; A metal net.

**Drawing #164**

363) 浮沓
(*ukigutsu*)
Literally "Floating Shoes". A type of floating aid.

364) 肌袴
(*hada bakama*)
Literally "Skin Trousers". This is worn as an inner-wear.

**365) 金覆輪鞍 (kin fukurin no kura)**
Bottom; A saddle with golden ornamental borders.

**Drawing #165**

**366) 貝鞍 (kaigura)**
Lacquered saddle.

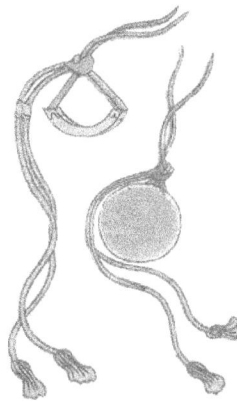

**367) 鏡鞍 (kagami shiode)**
Right; Tie-downs attached to the 4 sides of a saddle. This design has a mirror.

**Drawing #166**

**368) 取付 (toritsuke)**
Decorative tassels.

**369) 小四緒手 (ko shiode)**
Left; A simpler design of the tie-downs attached to a saddle.

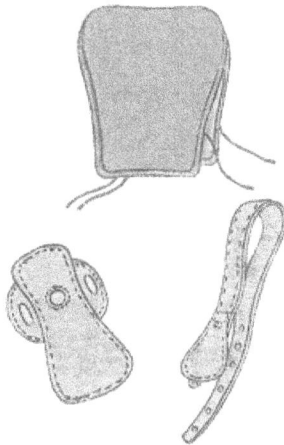

---

**370) 鞍帊 (kurapaku)**
Top; Saddle cloth.

**371) 逆鞖 (chikara gawa)**
Right; Stirrup straps. These are leather-straps that pass through slots in the saddle.

**372) 板馬韀 (itabasen)**
Left; This is a leather piece that you place on the saddle, which you will be sitting on. The "*chikara gawa*" strap passes through this piece. Read up on "*kura tsubo*".

**Drawing #167**

---

**373) 鏡鐙 (kagami abumi)**
Top; Literally "Mirror Stirrup". The front portion is made of reflective material. This is more apparent in the original colored book.

**374) 五六鐙 (goroku abumi)**
Right; Literally "Five Six Stirrup".

**Drawing #168**

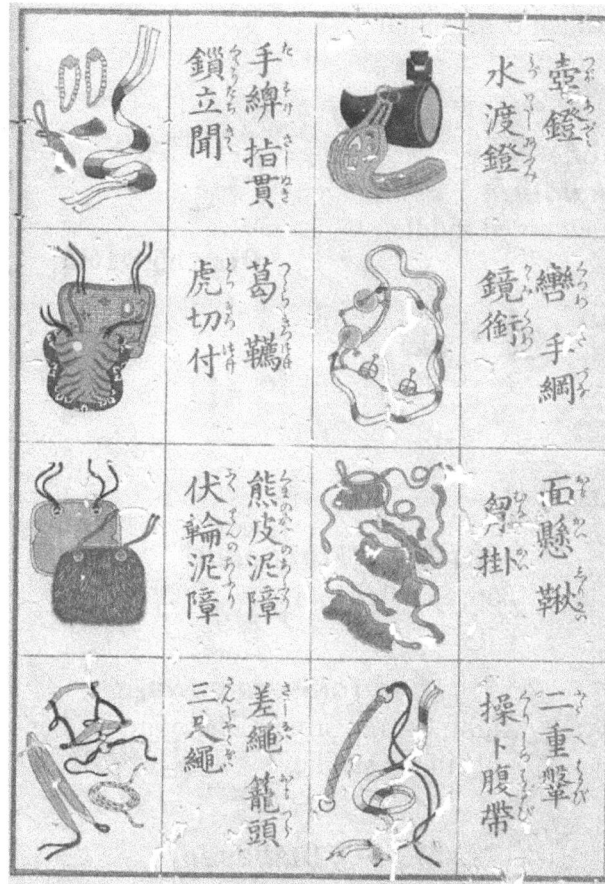

**Page 22 of the Drawings**

**Drawing #169**

375) 壺鐙
(*tsubo abumi*)
Pot-shaped stirrup.

376) 水渡鐙
(*mizuto abumi*)
Bottom; A stirrup
suitable for crossing
waters. Notice the
holes in its design.

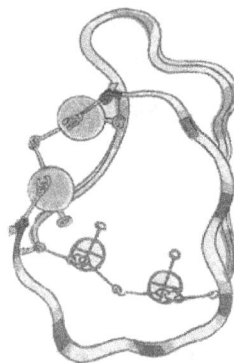

**Drawing #170**

377) 轡 (*kutsuwa*)
"Bit" for the horse.

378) 手綱 (*tazuna*)
Reins.

379) 鏡銜
(*kagami kutsuwa*)
Left; Literally "Mirror
Bit".

**380) 面懸 (*omogai*)**
Bridle, headgear for a horse.

**381) 鞦 (*shirigai*)**
Crupper. Attached to the saddle & looped under the horse's tail, so that the saddle won't slide forward.

**Drawing #171**

**382) 胸掛 (*munagai*)**
Breast strap for the horse.

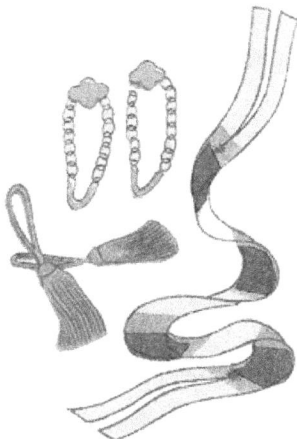

**Drawing #172**

**383) 二重鞏 (*niju ooobi*)**
Left; Abdomen strap for the horse. Double-ring design.

**384) 操卜腹帯 (*souto haraobi*)**
Similarly, an abdomen strap for horses, but a different fabric design.

---

**385) 轡 (*kutsuwa*)**
"Bit" for the horse.

**386) 手綱 (*tazuna*)**
Reins.

**387) 鏡銜 (*kagami kutsuwa*)**
Literally "Mirror Bit".

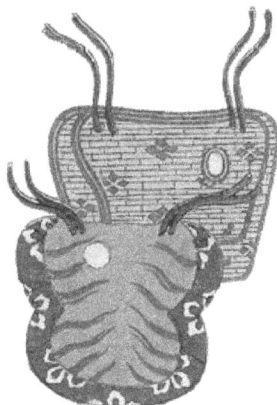

**Drawing #173**

---

**388) 葛鞦 (*tsuzura klttsuke*)**
This padding is placed on the back of a horse, to protect its skin from the saddle. AKA "*shita-kura*" or "*hadazuke*".

**389) 虎切付 (*tora kittsuke*)**
Tiger-skin design.

**Drawing #174**

**Drawing #175**

390) 熊皮泥障
(*kumanokawa aori*)
Bottom; Bear skin saddle flaps.

391) 伏輪泥障
(*fukurin no aori*)
Top; Saddle flaps with rounded design.

---

**Drawing #176**

392) 差縄 (*sashinawa*)
Halter, for restraining a horse.

393) 籠頭 (*omogai*)
Same as #380, but written with a different Kanji.

394) 三尺縄
(*sanjakunawa*)
Left; Two leather straps are attached to the bridle and bit, wrapping around the left and right side of the horse's neck. These help to prevent the bridle from slipping over the horse's ears.

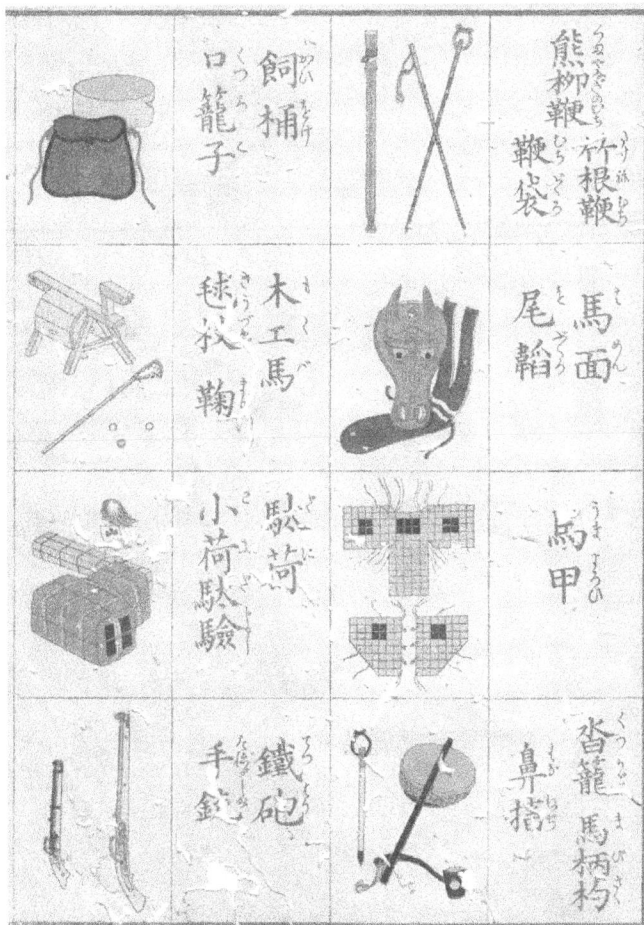

**Page 23 of the Drawings**

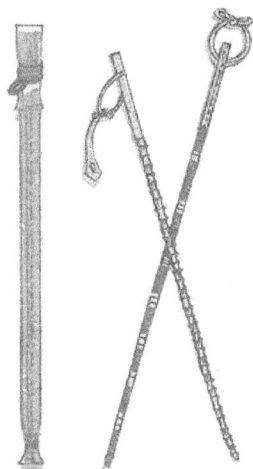

**Drawing #177**

### 395) 熊栁鞭 (*kumayanagi no muchi*)

Whip made of willow. A horse-rider will use this to whip the horse. The strap allows the whip to dangle at his wrist.

### 396) 竹根鞭 (*takene muchi*)

Bamboo whip.

### 397) 鞭袋 (*muchi bukuro*)

Right; Fabric bag for the whip.

**398) 馬面 (*bamen*)**
Face armour for horses.

**399) 尾韜 (*obukuro*)**
Fabric bag for the horse's tail.

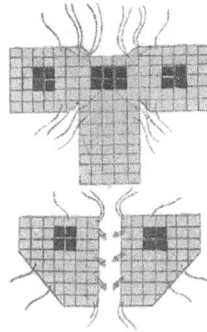

**Drawing #178**

**400) 馬甲 (*uma yoroi*)**
Body armour for horses.

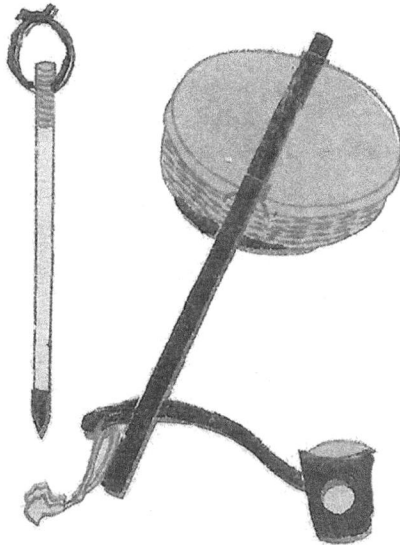

**Drawing #179**

**401) 沓籠 (*kutsukago*)**
A basket for containing footwear.

**402) 馬柄杓 (*mabishaku*)**
Bottom; A long handle ladle. Use for feeding water to horses.

**403) 鼻搔 (*hana neji*)**
Left; Also written as 鼻捩. This is used for controlling the long nose of a horse. Known as a "twitch" in Western equestry.

**Drawing #180**

**404) 飼桶 (*kaioke*)**
Bucket for horse feed.

**405) 口籠子 (*obukuro*)**
Basket used for feeding horses.

**Drawing #181**

**406) 木工馬 (*mokuba*)**
Top; Wooden horse.

**407) 毬杖 (*gicchou*)**
Middle; Polo stick.

**408) 鞠 (*mari*)**
Bottom; Balls.

**Drawing #182**

409) 駄荷
(*dani*)
Luggage load carried
by horses.

410) 小荷駄験
(*konidagen*)
Small parcels,
similarly carried by
horses.

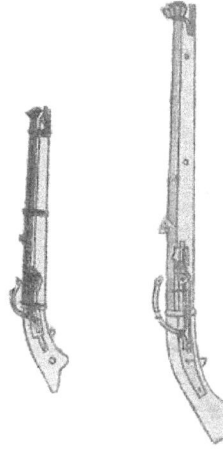

**Drawing #183**

411) 鐵砲
(*teppo*)
Right; Matchlock rifle.

412) 手銃
(*tezutsu*)
Left; Pistol.

**Drawing #184**

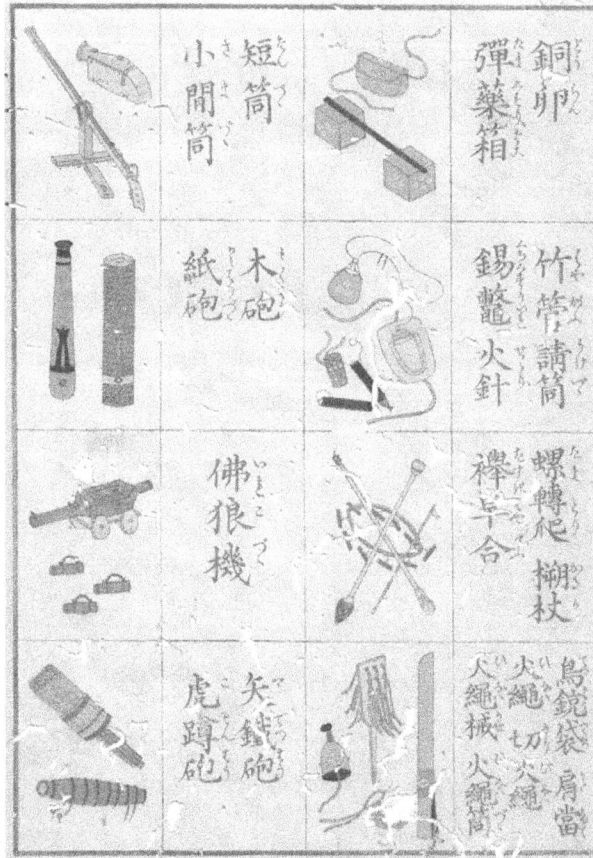

**Page 24 of the Drawings**

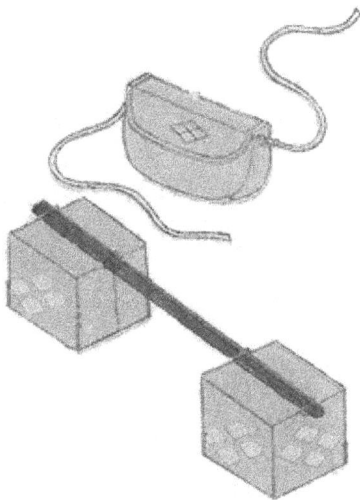

**Drawing #185**

413) 銅卵
**(*douran*)**
Metal pellets (as ammo for firearms).

414) 彈藥箱
**(*tama kusuri bako*)**
Container for firepowder.

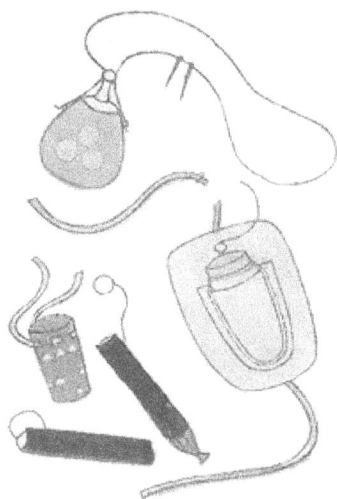

**Drawing #186**

## 415) 竹菅請筒 *(takegan ukezutsu)*

Right; Holder for bamboo tube.

## 416) 錫鼈 *(shakubetsu)*

Top; This was mentioned in Ming Dynasty General *Qi Ji-Guang*'s book, "*Lian Bing Shi Ji*". It is basically a little container for fire-powder, made of tin and shaped like a turtle.

## 417) 火針 *(hibari)*

Literally "Fire Needle".

---

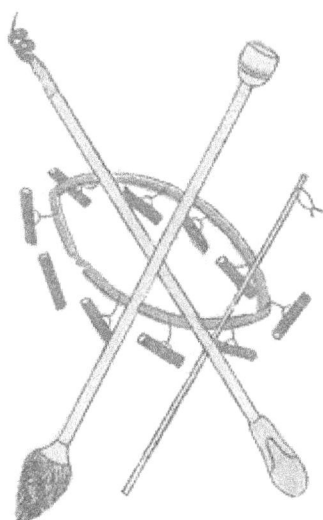

**Drawing #187**

## 418) 螺轉爬 *(tamatori)*

See the curly screwy tip at the top-left? This is possibly for retrieving stuck pellets in the barrel. This is my best guess, based on the Hiragana characters. "*Tama*" = pellets. "*Tori*" = retrieve.

## 419) 搠杖 *(sakujou)*

Also mentioned in Ming Dynasty General *Qi*'s book. After pouring fire-powder down the rifle's barrel, this is a stick that you will insert into the barrel and press hard to compress the fire-powder and make sure it's tightly packed.

## 420) 襷早合 *(tasuki hayagou)*

Middle; Rather than having to pour the fire-powder first, then load in the pellets, a "*hayagou*" is a pre-packed 'bullet' to save you the trouble. Here we see several being tied to a rope that you can carry easily.

**Drawing #188**

**421) 鳥銃袋 (*choujuu bukuro*)**
Right; Fabric bag for the rifle.

**422) 肩當 (*kata-ate*)**
Shoulder-guard.

**423) 火繩 (*hinawa*)**
Bottom; Coil; Literally "fire-rope".
For igniting the gun.

**424) 切火繩 (*kiribinawa*)**
Bottom; A single thread beside the
coil. This has been cut and prepared
for usage.

**425) 火繩械 (*hinawa kase*)**
Top; A tool for storing multiple "fire-
ropes" that has been cut and prepared.

**426) 火繩筒 (*hinawa zutsu*)**
Left; A tube for the "fire-rope".

---

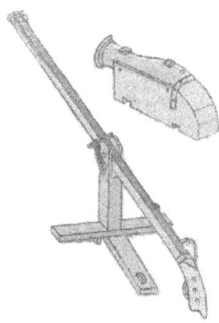

**Drawing #189**

**427) 短筒
(*tanzutsu*)**
Literally "Short
Cannon".

**428) 小間筒
(*komazutsu*)**
Literally "Narrow
Cannon". Note the
long narrow barrel,
like a sniper rifle.

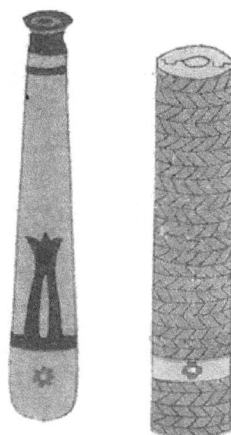

**Drawing #190**

**429) 木砲
(*mokupou*)**
Literally "Wooden
Cannon".

**430) 紙砲
(*kamizutsu*)**
Literally "Paper
Cannon".

**Drawing #191**

### 431) 佛狼機 (*futsurouki*)

Also written as "仏狼機". First found in Ming Dynasty China, imported from the Portugese.

The 3 small pieces below are the pre-packed ammunition, that you can load into this cannon to fire. After firing, simply replace it with a new one, thus allowing faster reload.

### 432) 矢鐵砲 (*yateppou*)

Top; Literally "Arrow Cannon".

### 433) 虎蹲砲 (*kosonpou*)

Bottom; Literally "Tiger Squatting Cannon", from Ming Dynasty China.

Lightweight and easily carried around, you can stab the spikes at the bottom into the ground to stabilize the cannon anywhere in the field.

The spikes are also detachable from the cannon, and can be attached on only when deploying it.

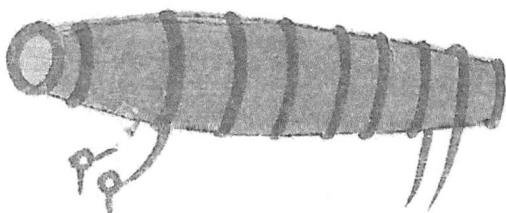

**Drawing #192**

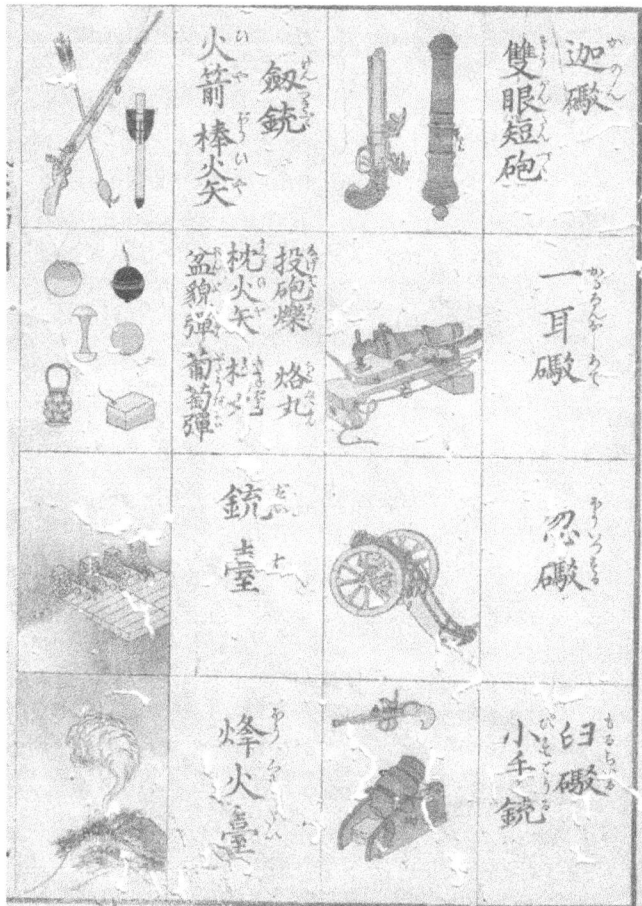

**Page 25 of the Drawings**

**Drawing #193**

### 434) 迦礮 (*ka'non*)
The hiragana literally reads "cannon".
Also written as "加農砲", or "カノン砲".

### 435) 雙眼短砲 (*sougan tanzutsu*)
Left; Literally "Double Eyed Short Cannon".
Observe the design of its "sights".

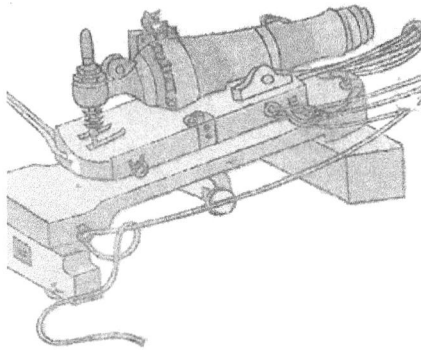

**Drawing #194**

### 436) 一耳礮
**(*kata mimi hou*)**
Literally "Single Ear Cannon".
Most cannons have 2 "ears", protrusion that allows it to be rested on a frame, and swivel up and down.

It appears that this only has one "ear" at the rear, which allows you to calibrate it to aim higher or lower.

---

**Drawing #195**

### 437) 忽礮
**(*houitsu hou*)**
Literally "Howitzer Cannon", written in Hiragana.

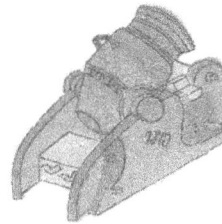

**Drawing #196**

### 438) 臼礮
**(*kyuuhou*)**
Bottom; A type of short cannon.

### 439) 小手銃
**(*pisutoru*)**
Top; Literally "Pistol" written in Hiragana.

---

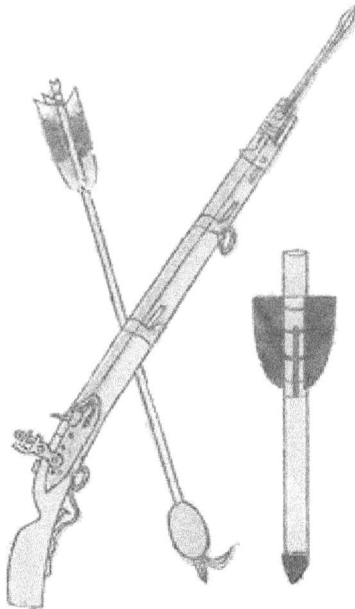

**Drawing #197**

### 440) 劔銃
**(*kenjuu*)**
Spear gun.

### 441) 火箭
**(*hiya*)**
Literally "Fire Arrow". Shot via bows.

### 442) 棒火矢
**(*bohiya*)**
Literally "Stick Fire Arrow".

**443) 投砲爍 (nage houroku)**
Literally "Hand-thrown Explosive", aka Grenade.

**444) 烙丸 (rakugan)**
Literally "Burning Pill".

**445) 枕火矢 (makura hiya)**
Literally "Pillow Fire Arrow". Possibly a hand-thrown weapon that you'd keep at bed-side.

**446) 杵丸 (kine dama)**
Literally "Pounder Pill". Possibly the middle-left.

**447) 盆貌彈 (bonbou tama)**
Literally "Basin Bomb".

**448) 葡萄彈 (budou dama)**
Bottom-left; Literally "Grapes Bomb", several small bombs cluster into a bundle.

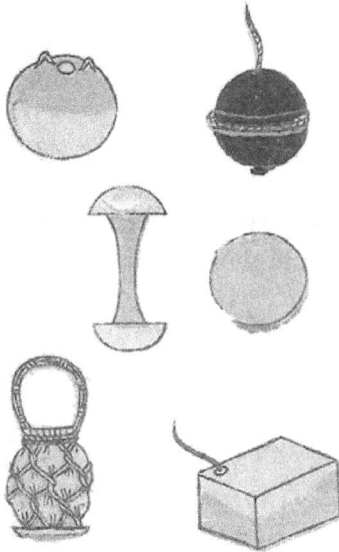

**Drawing #198**

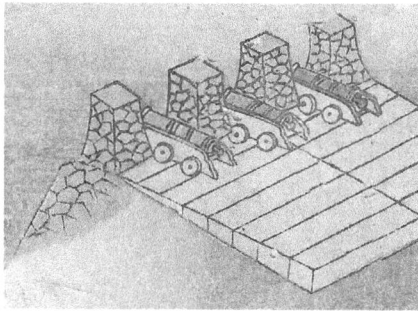

**Drawing #199**

**449) 銃臺 (judai)**
Literally "Cannon Platform".

**Drawing #200**

**450) 烽火臺 (houkadai)**
Smoke signals on high grounds.

# Thank You

It took a lot of time and effort to research and find out about each and every weapon or item showcased in this antique book. For instance, there are several items which you cannot type into Google to research. In order to find out more, I had to refer to other antique military manuals, both Chinese & Japanese.

Although this is supposed to be a Japanese book, there are some items which are of Chinese origin. But this is not surprising, considering that both cultures had a lot of exchanges through the centuries.

If you are looking for a 1:1 replica of this antique 200 drawings book, please visit:

- **www.Gekiken.org**
- or **www.SamuraiBookshop.com**
- Or you can also email me at: **GekikenORG@gmail.com**.

With the antique replica, you will be able to hold an exact copy in your hands, with all the drawings in **full color**! Who knows, maybe you'll spot some minor details that may reveal some new interesting information.

I hope this book will be useful and serve as a good reference in your study of ancient Japanese warfare and culture.

Sincerely,

Jack Chen

www.ingramcontent.com/pod-product-compliance
Lightning Source LLC
Chambersburg PA
CBHW081340090426
42737CB00017B/3227

9789811154089